THE

DIRECTORY

THE

DIRECTORY

by

GEORGES LEFEBVRE

Translated from the French by
ROBERT BALDICK

VINTAGE BOOKS
A Division of Random House
New York

CONTENTS

FOREWORD

Albert Mathiez died on February 25, 1932, in his chair at the Sorbonne, where in spite of growing ill health he had insisted on giving his lecture at the usual time. He was only fifty-eight; his activity was greater than ever and his premature death deprived us of masterly works which he had been maturing for a long time. There is not one of his countless readers who is not aware of the irreparable loss suffered by French history.

Of all his undertakings, the one dearest to his heart was undoubtedly that history of the French Revolution of which he had already published three volumes. After taking it up to the ninth of Thermidor, he was getting ready to continue it. His book on the Thermidorian reaction, likewise published by Monsieur Jacques Max Leclerc, a work which sheds new light on many aspects of the history of that period, shows how carefully he had prepared, as always, for his next task. But he did not have time to begin the volume for which we were all waiting.

Like Monsieur Jacques Max Leclerc, the editor of the Collection Armand Colin felt that it would be regrettable to leave his work unfinished, and he invited me to continue it. When I accepted this invitation I did so with a full awareness of the difficulty of the task, and I beg my readers to believe that if I undertook this task it was not in any spirit of presumption. Nor was it with the intention of abdicating my personal opinions in order to present nothing but a pastiche. In agreement with the publisher and the editor of the Collection, I simply felt that in continuing the work of Albert Mathiez we should be paying his memory an homage which would have pleased him.

GEORGES LEFEBVRE

NOTE: *This edition has been revised and corrected by Albert Soboul.*

THE DIRECTORY

CHAPTER ONE

Thermidorians and Directorials

On 4 Brumaire, Year IV (October 26, 1795), the Convention broke up; the Thermidorians abandoned power and, right away, took it back again under cover of the Constitution of Year III. Thermidorians and Directorials were all one: the same men, the same ends, the same means. They had outlawed the Jacobins and announced the return to liberty; but in destroying the organization of Year II, they had also ruined the *assignat*, abandoned the common people to the miseries of inflation, reduced the armies to impotence, and revived the hopes of the counterrevolution. Then they had forced the electors to choose two-thirds of the new deputies from the Convention, broken the insurrection of the thirteenth of Vendémiaire, and revived the exceptional laws against the émigrés and the clergy. The whole history of the Directory lives up to these portents.

In repudiating democracy, the new Constitution gave political power back to the bourgeoisie and to the notables, by property qualification for suffrage, and, with economic liberty, a pre-eminent position to society. True, in order to be a *citoyen actif*, it was enough to pay a direct tax of any kind, but in order to be appointed an elector one had to be the owner or tenant of an estate or a house for which the land-tax, it seems, was thirty or forty francs. It was these electors—about 30,000 at the most—who chose the representatives. This regime the Thermidorians knew to be threatened, on the one hand by the Jacobins and *sansculottes*, and on the other hand by the counterrevolutionaries.

It was to the former that they had given most thought. A considerable number of measures had been taken with a view to preventing any popular movement. There was no longer a mayor or a commune of Paris; the big towns were divided among several municipalities, and their central office, which was in charge of the police, was appointed by the department, subject to confirmation by the government. In Paris, a military guard surrounded the Directory and the Councils. The latter admitted only a restricted audience and could go into secret session. What is more, the Council of the Ancients, if it thought fit, could move the government outside the capital. The clubs were still authorized, but could no longer be anything but public gatherings, deprived of all means of action; they were forbidden to affiliate with one another, to correspond with one another, or to send deputations and collective petitions. Moreover, the Legislature could authorize domiciliary visits and suspend the freedom of the press for a year with nothing to prevent it from repeating these measures. Better still, the Directory could have individuals suspected of conspiracy arrested without intervention by the law, in other words by *lettre de cachet*, on condition that they be questioned within twenty-four hours and handed over, if there were sufficient grounds, to the appropriate judge; but they had no possibility of appeal.

Finally, once the Constitution had been passed, the Montagnard members of the Convention indicted or arrested during the White Terror were declared ineligible. The amnesty granted on 4 Brumaire for actions "connected with the Revolution" did not benefit them; moreover, its vagueness placed the terrorists at the mercy of the courts and the juries, henceforth composed of their enemies, and also left them exposed to civil law-suits for damages.

In spite of everything, the bourgeoisie did not feel reassured, and if its fear turned into an electoral maneuver against the "terrorists," "exclusives," "anarchists," "brigands," and "drinkers of blood," this fear was nonetheless sincere. What it dreaded was not only arbitrary arrests and summary executions, but also the resurrection of the popular government which had deprived the notables of power, treated the rich with suspicion and helped the poor. In its eyes, political democracy would lead to social democracy, as a prelude to the "agrarian law" and the division of property. The Directory had scarcely been installed before Dauchy would declare to the Five Hundred that "graduated taxation is the real germ of an agrarian law"; a little later Pons de l'Aveyron would say sententiously: "The poor man's interest is his neighbor's wealth"; on 18 Fructidor, la Revellière would prefer to expose himself to the "daggers of the Royalists" rather than appeal to the Faubourg Antoine. "Social" fear dominated the history of the Directory and served as a pretext for the eighteenth of Brumaire just as it later dominated the history of the Second Republic and served as a pretext for the second of December.

However the Thermidorians were just as determined to prevent a Royalist restoration, which, they maintained, would call in question the social achievement of the Revolution. Now the enemies of the Republic were still in arms: Condé's army was encamped opposite Alsace; Charette had taken the field again and was waiting for the Comte d'Artois, who had landed on the island of Yeu; their confederates had carried out the Vendémiaire rebellion and were conspiring everywhere; supported by foreign governments, they would remain formidable until a general peace reduced them to their own strength. Against them too, combat measures remained in force.

The émigrés, whose list remained open, were banished for life and liable to the death penalty on identification if they were caught carrying arms or if they re-entered France. They were deprived of all civic rights and their property was confiscated and sold. Yet in Year III, a good many of them had come back, and got the Thermidorian authorities to strike them off the list temporarily. Then again, when the Federalists who had been outlawed after the thirty-first of May had been rehabilitated, those who had been listed as émigrés had been struck off; this was an open door and the citizens of Toulon who had handed

6

their town over to the English had taken advantage of it. Having accepted the idea that people could have emigrated innocently and out of fear, the Thermidorians had also amnestied the Alsatians, who had followed the Austrians in their retreat, provided that they were artisans or farm workers, and excluding nobles and priests. But after Quiberon, severity had prevailed: the Toulon offenders had been outlawed once more; the Constitution forbade any new exceptions; the émigrés who had been provisionally struck off the list were excluded from public office.

The émigrés were not the only ones to be affected. Those individuals of whom they were the heirs presumptive could not dispose of their property, because the Republic had appropriated in advance the successions which might devolve upon the fugitives during the fifty years after their listing, when, deprived of their civic rights, they were incapable of inheriting and doubly so if they died before their parents. On 12 Floréal, Year III (May 1, 1795), the latter had been instructed to redeem their debt by sharing an anticipated succession with the Republic, thus liquidating their succession before it had been opened. Then the Right, protesting at the responsibility imputed to the émigrés' relatives, made these judicial contradictions a pretext for setting aside all this legislation. After the thirteenth of Vendémiaire, the relatives of émigrés—husband, father and stepfather, son and grandson, uncle and nephew —had nonetheless been affected by it in another way: the law of 3 Brumaire, Year IV (October 25, 1795) excluded them from public office.

Finally, the counterrevolutionaries who had not emigrated also had their share of trouble: the Vendeans, the Chouans, and the Vendémiaire rebels were handed over to military commissions; the same law of 3 Brumaire was applied to all those who, in the primary and electoral assemblies, had put forward or signed seditious motions, and thus to the ostentatious supporters of the Vendémiairists; moreover, the measures which threatened the Jacobins served a double purpose and were aimed equally at the Royalists.

The priests were not spared either. Those who, ordered to take the oath of November 27, 1790, had refused or retracted—the non-juring clergy—had been deported, or, to be more precise, banished; if they had insisted on remaining in France, they were liable to be transported to Guiana; those who returned exposed themselves to the death penalty, simply on identification. Sentence of transportation was also pronounced on all other secular and regular ecclesiastics, even constitutional priests, if they had refused the "little oath" of loyalty to liberty and equality of August 14, 1792, or if they were denounced as agitators by six citizens in their department. Priests who were infirm or over sixty years of age were excepted, but were punished by compulsory retirement. These laws had fallen into abeyance in the course of Year III and the Constitution had made no mention of them; the deportees had returned like the émigrés, and the priests who had gone into hiding had reappeared. But the law of 3 Brumaire had revived this harsh legislation.

The Thermidorians had laid themselves open to cutting sarcasm by retaining this legislative arsenal while raging and fuming at the terrorists, especially since, as always happens, these laws, when not completely ineffective, were unfairly generalized. Not all terrorists were criminals, and not all democrats were terrorists. Similarly, not all émigrés were traitors, and not all non-juring priests counterrevolutionaries. But there was more to it than that: Jacobins and Royalists—at least some of the latter—were, for the Thermidorians, interchangeable allies.

Against the Royalists, the Republicans had formed a solid front, as had been seen on the thirteenth of Vendémiaire. It was only natural that in exchange for their support the Jacobins should ask that at least the amnesty should be faithfully interpreted, that they should be admitted to public office and that their leaders should be returned to them.

Inversely, it was in vain that the Thermidorians affected to treat all Royalists as counterrevolutionaries: they nonetheless found support in their ranks against democracy. The Monarchists were just as divided as the Republicans. The former Feuillants were willing to recall Louis XVIII only if he accepted the Constitution of 1791 in a suitably revised form, whereas the King had publicly declared his support for the Absolutists who wanted to re-establish the *ancien régime*. That is why they had resigned themselves to passing the Constitution of Year III, and, in spite of the decree of the two-thirds and of the thirteenth of Vendémiaire, they were prepared to respect it until such time as the restoration of the monarchy became possible. But it went without saying that in exchange they demanded that the Jacobins be outlawed once more, that all official positions be given to "decent people," and that the exceptional laws be repealed or at least considerably amended.

Thermidorians and Directorials were quite willing to be indulgent towards docile Jacobins, and they never stopped urging the Royalist bourgeoisie to join them in order to consolidate the conservative Republic; but they still refused to give up the exceptional measures. They have been generally praised for their attitude towards the Jacobins, but their distrust of the "decent people" has been severely criticized. Yet it is easy to explain: first of all, by prejudices and interests of a personal nature. The Republican bourgeoisie was usually of low extraction and of modest or too recent fortunes; the Monarchist bourgeoisie, on the other hand, represented inherited wealth; its connections and way of life drew it towards the aristocracy. Then again, the blood of Louis XVI, or at least the tenth of August, separated Republicans and Royalists; what would be the fate of the former if the latter won the day? Moreover, was it likely that they would remain content with a Republic without Republicans? The experiment of Year III was conclusive: they had been given a free rein and the country had found itself on the verge of a restoration. It was not for nothing that the Thermidorians accused the Constitutionalists of complicity with the Absolutists: in control of the Republic, they would have left it defenseless; they found violent action repugnant, but would have allowed it; they did not want an invasion, but would have resigned themselves to it; they had negotiated with foreign countries before the tenth of August and they would take their money. The work of the Revolution remained unfinished, and, if it was to resist all attacks, it needed time. Yet the fact remains that the Thermidorians wanted the Republic to live while excluding those who had founded it; they wanted it to be bourgeois while refusing to give any power to a great part of the bourgeoisie; they wanted it to remain despotic while calling itself liberal.

They could obtain help in sustaining these paradoxes only by the offer of places and the bait of profitable business.

To tell the truth, their opponents, if they had dropped their masks, would not have appealed to the voters and electors. Nobody cared very much about Louis XVIII, and as for returning to the *ancien régime*, there could be no question of that. On the other hand, people's minds were no longer obsessed with the "aristocratic plot," now that the French armies were victorious and the Coalition shattered; as a result, nobody recalled anything of the Jacobin dictatorship except the memory of its demands and its severity. But the Thermidorians were no less unpopular than their rivals. The French people were weary. Having carried out the Revolution to be happy, they wanted to live in peace and longed for the war to come to an end so that they might have fewer taxes to pay, and not have to go and fight. Fundamentally, what they blamed the Jacobins for was their intransigence which, carrying the Revolution to extremes, had imposed too many sacrifices. Had the Thermidorians done much better? Bankruptcy was imminent, famine was rampant, and the war went on.

Nor was this all. This longed-for peace depended, to a certain extent, on an agreement between the Republic and the Catholic Church, whose conflict kept civil war alive and brought discord even into individual families. The civic religion which had been proposed to the people did not appeal to them; the new calendar disturbed their daily life and they preferred to rest one day in seven rather than one day in ten. The Catholic revival was one of the most striking features of the time. Now, the Constitution confirmed the separation of Church and State, and, if it recog-

nized freedom of worship, it was on condition that the
rules governing religious worship were observed. The clergy
had to promise submission to the law and recognize the
French people as their lawful sovereign. Not all of them
were *soumissionnaires* and the schism between them had
become more complex. Moreover, the people were showing
increasing irritation at the ban on all demonstrations outside the churches, such as processions and pilgrimages, in-
scriptions and crosses, the wearing of ecclesiastical dress,
and the ringing of bells. This was not how they understood
freedom of worship, and accordingly they broke the law.
Most of the time, the local authorities shut their eyes; if
they intervened they encountered resistance. There can be
no doubt whatever that, although the Thermidorians did
not close the churches, they were as eager as the *sans-
culottes* to de-Christianize France, because they regarded
the Revolution and Catholicism as incompatible. The majority of the French people were not of this opinion. Yet
those who criticize the Thermidorians on this score usually
fail to recall that many of the non-juring clergy upheld the
same point of view and put their religion at the service of their politics; some took up arms with the Chouans.
The Thermidorians were convinced that, far from dis-
arming them, concessions would make them more dangerous than ever.

Accordingly, if the opposing sides refrained from advocating monarchical or revolutionary government, they had
no scruples about attacking the rulers of the day, whom
they held responsible for everything that was amiss. It was
the Royalists who obtained the readier hearings; they argued that peace was impossible as long as power remained
in the hands of the regicides and the persecutors of religion,

who had made the sovereigns of Europe irreconcilable by extending France to her so-called natural frontiers and by threatening every throne with propaganda for universal revolution. Consequently it was another paradox on the part of the Thermidorians to return to the electoral system with nothing to offer but bankruptcy and war, especially at a time when, with many of the best patriots in the army, the absentees, the deserters, the rebels and the émigrés who had returned to France would rush to the ballot boxes. It was yet another paradox to have ordered annual elections to replace one-third of the Councils, half the municipalities, and one-fifth of the Directory and the departments; the partial character of the change only slightly reduced the inconvenience of its frequency, especially as re-eligibility was limited. In the midst of war, the government, exposed to continual agitation, would have neither stability nor permanence.

The electoral methods increased the danger. To choose the electors, the *citoyens actifs* met in cantons and voted when their names were called; they therefore had to travel to the seat of the canton and then wait in patience. As the system provided for repeated ballots, the assembly could last for several days, and because of the considerable number of absentees, a determined minority could win out by perseverance. It was the assembly which decided arguments about the admission of *citoyens actifs* and the eligibility of candidates; how could it be prevented from degenerating into a club? A party that did not shrink from violent methods could gain control of it. An appeal to the courts and to the Legislature was permitted, but it had not been possible to make it suspensive. The only course open to malcontents was to secede and go off to deliberate somewhere else; in this way there could be two or more lists of electors in competition. There was nothing to prevent things taking the same turn at the electoral assembly.

These methods benefited the extremist parties. To favor the White Terror, the Royalists had excluded the Republicans; if the Royalists were outlawed once more, the electoral system could benefit the Jacobins. The Thermidorians had provided against the danger by means of the decree of the two-thirds, which had assured them of a majority until the elections of Year V. But would a respite of eighteen months be sufficient to heal wounds and win over the electors? It was unlikely, and if not, only a *coup d'état* would be able to maintain the bourgeois republic; imitating the Jacobin Republic after having denounced it, it would return to a dictatorship—and a dictatorship very different from that of Year II. Since there could be no question of support from the common people, it could only be installed by the army. Then it would be challenged again every year: an annual *coup d'état* would make a stable government impossible. Above all, it would have to do without the Committee of Public Safety, the government's powers being so organized that their division would be inevitable.

The Thermidorian bourgeoisie in fact was not only afraid of democracy and Royalism; it also wanted to guard against the omnipotence of the State, and, to that end, had been careful to achieve a multiplication and balance of powers. The Legislature was divided into two Councils which could only communicate through *"messages"*: the Five Hundred, aged at least thirty, and the Ancients, 250 in number, aged at least forty and married men or widowers. The Five Hundred had the initiative: they passed "resolutions" which the Ancients turned into "laws" if they thought fit. The Thermidorians believed that they had done everything to prevent an audacious minority from imposing its will: positions were drawn by lot, the committee was appointed for only a month at a time, and no permanent commission could be set up. The executive was entrusted to a Directory of five members, aged at least forty, and to the ministers appointed by the Directory. The Treasury, the Accounts Department, the judges, and the High Court constituted yet other powers.

All were independent of one another. The Directory could not adjourn the Councils, still less dissolve them; it was entitled to ask them to pass a law, but forbidden to present them with the text; access to the Councils was barred to it except by means of *messages*. Inversely, if the Legislature elected the Directors—the Ancients choosing them from a list of ten drawn up by the Five Hundred—it had no means of exerting pressure on them except by indicting them; it had no contact with the ministers. As for the judges, they were elected. Everything was arranged so that the constituted authorities, acting as checks on one another, were incapable of oppressing the citizens.

But everything was also arranged so that discussion should be slow and execution hampered. Yet, as in 1793 the Republic was engaged in civil and foreign war, and it was just as important for the government to be able to act speedily and energetically. The danger had apparently not escaped the Thermidorians' notice, for they had granted the Directory considerable powers: the right to issue decrees; control of foreign affairs and the ability to conclude treaties, even secret ones; the choice of generals and the conduct of the war; and the control of the police and local administration. The latter had been reorganized in such a way as to condense its authority and strengthen government control. There was no longer a departmental council, but only a central administration of five members. The district had been abolished, as had the general council of the commune; towns of 5,000 inhabitants and more had only municipal offices; the smaller communes retained only an agent and his assistant, the municipality consisting of an assembly of these agents at the seat of the canton. The Directory could quash without appeal the deliberations of the local administrations, dismiss their members and replace them if all their seats fell vacant at the same time, the vacancies otherwise being filled by co-optation. It attached to each administration a commissioner who was subject to dismissal. The departmental commissioner, a permanent official beside temporary, elected officials, in direct correspondence with the government, directing the committees and giving orders to the other commissioners, foreshadowed the Prefect of the future.

However, this was a long way from the centralization of the Jacobins or the Consulate. It was difficult for the central commissioner, by himself, to keep a close watch on the municipalities, of which there were so many, often far apart. The assessment and collection of taxes remained in the hands of the elected administrations. The Directory had no control over the Treasury. In the courts, it was represented only by a commissioner who could take no part in the prosecution, which was left to the gendarmerie officer, the justice of the peace, and the director of the indictment jury. Here, the difference from the system of Year

II was obvious: short of setting up countless military commissions, the Directory lacked "coercive force."

But worst of it was that there was nothing to guarantee co-operation between the Directory and the Councils; rivalry between the Executive and the Legislature is an inherent evil of the representative system. The Directory's powers were considerable and circumstances made it necessary to increase them still further. The Councils often paralyzed it by their inertia, yet never ceased to be jealous of it. The Convention had overthrown the great Committee of Public Safety to escape from its influence. The Directory of Year VII would have its ninth of Thermidor. The nature of things imposed a return to revolutionary dictatorship, but the Constitution of Year III, in the form the Thermidorians had conceived it, forced them to exercise that dictatorship ineffectively.

Could it be changed? Yes, no doubt it could, but a delay of seven years was required for any proposal to come into effect. Another *coup d'état* would be necessary to revise the Constitution of Year III, and it would not survive the operation.

CHAPTER TWO

The Beginning of the Directory

The electors had observed the decree of the two-thirds, but only 379 members of the Convention had been re-elected, because several had been elected simultaneously in a large number of departments. Provision had been made for this eventuality. They gathered together in the "Electoral Assembly of France" and filled the vacant seats. After the new Third had made its entry, the Councils took their seats, the Ancients in the Tuileries in the hall which the Convention had just left, and the Five Hundred in the Riding School, where the Constituent Assembly, the Legislative

Assembly, and the Convention in its early days had sat. In Year VI, they would move into the former Palais-Bourbon.

Generally speaking, the electors had rejected the Jacobins and chosen the mildest members of the Convention; Royalists like Boissy d'Anglas, Lanjuinais and Henry-Larivière had been elected in over thirty departments. The choices of the Electoral Assembly of France had fallen somewhat further left; the new Third, further right. On the whole, only a few Jacobins had survived; the majority in the Directory was extremely varied; there were some Montagnards, Merlin, Barras, Tallien; a good many members of the Plain in the Convention, Sieyès, Ramel, Letourneur; some Girondins, La Revellière, Louvet, Chénier; and some members of the Constituent and Legislative Assemblies, Creuzé-Latouche and Lecoulteux. A small group hostile to the exceptional laws—Thibaudeau, Doulcet, Cambacérès—formed a link with the Constitutional Monarchists, who included Dupont de Nemours, Mathieu Dumas, Portalis, Tronson-Ducoudray, Pastoret, Dumolard, Vaublanc and Barbé-Marbois. Further right was the extremist opposition, which was also mixed; next to Gibert-Desmolières and Boissy d'Anglas, there were Henry-Larivière, organizers of the White Terror such as Cadroy and Isnard, and Job Aymé, a real Chouan and an auxiliary of the Marquis de Lestang who had recently been shot. These Councils were full of capable, educated men who would figure in large numbers in the personnel of the Consulate, but there were few orators among them; neither Sieyès nor Carnot could speak well; Portalis was known as the "warm water tap" and Dumolard as the "overflow of the Isère."

The choice of the Directors was of major interest, and,

on the morrow of the thirteenth of Vendémiaire, the majority allowed no breach to be made in its numbers. The members of the Convention in the Five Hundred got together to draw up a list of second-rate individuals, except for five regicides whom the Ancients would be obliged to choose; at the sitting, the Right only managed to slip Cambacérès into the second rank. In the Council of the Ancients, protests were made at the maneuver, but the Five were elected. They were La Revellière, Letourneur, Reubell, Sieyès and Barras. Sieyès refused: he had quarreled with Reubell, and, furious at having had his project for a Constitution rejected, was biding his time. Carnot was elected in his place.

La Revellière, the son of a Poitou notary, transplanted to Angers by his marriage, had been elected by that town to the Constituent Assembly and to the Convention. A Girondin, he had been obliged to go into hiding during the Terror, and his brother had been guillotined. He was therefore passionately hostile to the Jacobins, and as conservative as any Constitutional Monarchist; but he differed from them, not only in his indefectible attachment to the Republican form of government, but in his violent anticlericalism and a pronounced liking for propaganda warfare. Honest, disinterested, and living a modest family life, he was unfortunately a mediocrity and lacked prestige, especially as he was slightly deformed.

The Alsatian Reubell, a capable self-assertive man, had more personality. A barrister before the Revolution, he too had sat in the Constituent Assembly and the Convention; he had been a Montagnard and, according to Barras, he once said that he had never blamed Robespierre for anything but being too gentle. To tell the truth, his conduct at

Mainz had aroused the suspicions of the Committee of Public Safety, and this had driven him into opposition. His was the steadiest head in the Directory and he also stood out as the advocate of the natural frontiers, especially that of the Rhine. There were doubts about his probity, but no proof to back them up.

The Vicomte Paul de Barras was, like Mirabeau, a corrupt, dissolute noble who had thrown himself into the Revolution to seek his fortune. As a member of the Convention he had behaved as an extreme terrorist at Marseilles and Toulon and, recalled to Paris, had turned against the Committee of Public Safety. This handsome man, a former officer with an imposing manner, offered a striking contrast with his commoner colleagues, but nobody had any illusions about the "King of the Republic"; it was known that he made money out of everything and surrounded himself with a crowd of dishonest individuals and loose women. All the same, he was probably sincere when he said that the most important thing was to "save the men of the Revolution," or showed a penchant for annexations and propaganda. In any case, since he had saved the Convention in Thermidor and Vendémiaire, it was felt that he was an inevitable choice.

Carnot, as a member of the Committee of Public Safety, had nearly been outlawed with his colleagues, and he was repugnant to La Revellière as also to the Right; Reubell hated the despot in him and Barras the honest man. The majority did not like him either, imagining that he would protect the Jacobins; but it had considered him necessary to the conduct of the war. He had some strange surprises in store for one and all. Letourneur, a former engineering officer like himself, acted as his auxiliary.

Thus the Directory, right from the start, was as divided as the Committee of Public Safety in its last days; on the one hand, Carnot and Letourneur; on the other, La Revellière and Reubell, who moreover were far from being always in agreement; and then Barras, on whom no one could rely, since he could be bought and thought of nothing but himself.

The Directors installed themselves uncomfortably in the Luxembourg, which was completely unfurnished and delapidated, having served as a prison for over a year. Since the Treasury was empty, it took several months before they could cut a figure there. Each of them presided in turn for three months. A certain specialization was established among them: the conduct of the war fell to Carnot, foreign affairs to Reubell and education to La Revellière. They shared the departments among themselves when organizing local administration. The Constitution granted them a secretary, who was Lagarde, a former councilor to the bailliage of Lille and secretary of the department of the Nord. His position was an extremely important one, for it was through him that business was divided up among the ministers and returned to the Directory; the organization that he set up was retained by Bonaparte and became the Secretariat of State.

Six ministers were appointed to begin with: as Minister of the Interior, Bénézech, a capable man whom the Committee of Public Safety had employed, but who, married to an aristocrat, rapidly fell under suspicion on account of his manners and connections; as Minister of Finance, Faipoult, a former nobleman promptly replaced by Ramel-Nogaret, a regicide and brilliant financier who kept the post until Year VII; as Minister of Justice, Merlin de Douai, the author of the Law of Suspects and now an anti-Jacobin, a great worker and an eminent jurist, but lacking in character; as Minister of External Relations, Delacroix, another regicide, who was far from untalented but was little more than Reubell's clerk; as Minister of War, Aubert-Dubayet, for whom Carnot soon substituted Petiet, a former war commissioner and a good administrator; and finally, as Navy Minister, Admiral Truguet. Before long a seventh ministry was created, that of the Police, to which Merlin was appointed, his place as Minister of Justice being taken by Genissieu, a former member of the Convention.

The organization of the local authorities was much more difficult. The Directory had to appoint thousands of commissioners in a hurry. A great many electoral assemblies, for example that of the Seine, had not finished their task in the ten days allowed by the Constitution, and they were forbidden to meet in extraordinary session. Without raising many difficulties, the Councils instructed the Directory to fill the places in the central and municipal administrations which were vacant. As far as the judges were concerned, there was strong resistance, but it eventually subsided. As the Convention had postponed the election of the municipalities of the big towns, the Directory was similarly authorized to nominate them. It was a seemingly endless task, for there were countless refusals and resignations; moreover, the elections having been favorable to the Royalists, the number of dismissals increased. Admittedly, co-optation was used; but this was surely a ridiculous remedy when over half the members of an administration had disappeared. In such cases the Directory arrogated the choice of the replacements to itself, and it retained that choice, in spite of protests from the Councils. Thus, right from the start, its power grew considerably. To a great extent, it appointed the courts and the local administrations, as the Committees of the Convention had done and the Consuls would do. By its decrees, it promptly encroached on the legislative power, without the Councils ever trying to bar its way, although they never stopped complaining. And, in spite of everything, the composition of the courts and the administrations was never stable or satisfactory, partly because the members could not be paid, so that the Directory was never scrupulously obeyed.

Its task was unenviable. It had no financial resources, and although winter would bring hostilities on the frontier to a halt, disturbances were continuing at home. In Paris, which was still under military occupation, the commissions were trying the Vendémiaire rebels, two of whom were executed; Royalist demonstrations nonetheless continued in the streets, at the Café de Valois, and above all in the theaters; there, the Directory banned the *Réveil du peuple* and ordered the *Marseillaise* and other patriotic songs to be sung. The newspapers suppressed in Vendémiaire gradually reappeared; in the spring they had 150,000 subscribers, compared with 4,000 to the Republican papers. The Directory set up a Public Spirit Office to supervise them; it had some official papers of its own—the *Rédacteur* and the *Moniteur*—and subsidized others. In the southeast, where the Marquis de Lestang had been shot after occupying Avignon, the White Terror was still raging; the Directory supported the representatives sent there by the Convention, Fréron in Provence and Reverchon in Lyons. It did not take long to uncover a plot by Bésignan, a veteran of the counterrevolution in that region, and another aimed at delivering Besançon and the Comté into the hands of the Prince de Condé. The latter had been negotiating for a long time with Pichegru, who was in command of the Army of the Rhine and Moselle, but whose disastrous autumn campaign led to his replacement at the end of December. Yet it was the west that was giving most trouble. Charette waited in vain for a landing by the Comte d'Artois, who, at the end of October, had returned to England, but in January, 1796, Stofflet in his turn took up arms again. After Quiberon, Hoche had been put in supreme command, and on his advice the Directory had given him permission to let the laws on the clergy and religious worship fall into abeyance. But, contrary to legend, he pacified the region only by the use of great strength and severity. He surrounded it with lines of fortified posts and forced the peasants to surrender their arms in a series of raids which left them without any resources. Finally Stofflet and Charette were captured and shot, the former at Angers on February 25, 1796, and the latter at Nantes on March 29. After that, "Palluau's Vendée" had to be crushed in the Indre, and another insurrection in the Sancerrois. Then Hoche had to subjugate the Chouan leaders north of the Loire; Cadoudal and Guillemot, "the King of Bignan," in the Morbihan; Boisguy in Ille-et-Vilaine; Frotté in the Bocage Normand; and Scépeaux in the Maine. In June, the war was declared to be over, and the Army of the West was dissolved. But isolated bands continued to carry out murders and robberies.

Threatened in this way by the counterrevolution, the Directory, for some weeks, went on appealing to that union of Republicans which had been the order of the day since Vendémiaire. In its appointments, it gave the Jacobins a large place. It treated the Leftist press sympathetically, subsidizing Poultier's *Ami des Lois* and Duval's *Journal des hommes libres*. A holiday in commemoration of the twenty-first of January was ordained, and an oath of hatred for monarchy was imposed on public servants. Orders were given to enforce the laws against the clergy and the émigrés. Above all, no obstacle had been placed in the way of the re-opening of the clubs. The most important of the clubs, that of the Panthéon, inaugurated on 25 Brumaire, Year IV (November 16, 1795), soon had a thousand members. To begin with, it was deferential in its attitude to the government and showed a readiness to wait and see how it performed. Gracchus Babeuf, who had just resumed publication of his *Tribun du peuple*, in which he immediately declared war on the bourgeoisie, was condemned at first by the whole of the Leftist press.

In the Five Hundred, the Right fulminated most of all over the reinstatement of Jacobins in the local administrations, while the Left obtained the exclusion of the deputies who came within the provisions of the law of 3 Brumaire, notably Job Aymé. The result was often brawling worthy of the Convention. The majority remained fairly solid. In the case of the West Indian settlers who had taken refuge in the United States, and whom the Directory wanted to consider as émigrés, the Right only obtained an adjournment. As for the relatives of the émigrés, it could not prevent a revival of the division of anticipated successions, but succeeded in getting it declared optional.

However, circumstances gradually began to favor them. This was because the Jacobins had not been long in getting out of hand. They had humored the Directory only in the hope of carrying it with them, and they soon became impatient. Gradually they took the offensive under the in-

26

fluence of Darthé, Lebon's collaborator at Arras; of Lebois, the journalist on the *Orateur plébéien*; of Le Peletier, the brother of the murdered member of the Convention; of the Italian refugee Buonarroti; and of two members of the Convention who had been declared ineligible, Amar and Robert Lindet. As early as 14 Frimaire (December 5), a warrant had been issued for the arrest of Babeuf, who henceforth lived in hiding; Lebois was prosecuted; on 1 Pluviôse (January 21), Reubell declared menacingly in a speech: "Let good citizens be reassured." The Jacobin Club and the Leftist newspapers protested violently. The Directory took fright and broke completely with the Jacobins at the idea that they might be going to start an insurrection in the suburbs. For at this moment the *assignat* was in its death-throes, and in the depths of winter the common people were suffering terrible hardship.

CHAPTER THREE

The Monetary Crisis and the Conspiracy of the Equals

At the time the Directory was installing itself, inflation was entering its final period. The *assignat* of 100 francs was worth from fifteen to sixteen sous, and prices were rising hour by hour. The sale of national estates had to be suspended and a moratorium declared to save creditors from ruin. The Directory could not manage to get enough *assignats* printed during the night for the following day and found itself at the mercy of a strike. In less than four months, the issue had approximately doubled.

Yet the Left persisted in maintaining that the revolutionary currency could be put on its feet again; the Right, on the other hand, declared that bankruptcy was inevitable, with tremendous benefit to its propaganda. Behind the political conflict it was possible to catch a glimpse of the social antagonism: the Left wanted the rich to be compelled to pay a graduated tax which would reduce the amount of the "token"; the Right wanted to spare them this sacrifice and satisfy the bankers. In any case, the special interest of bulls and bears compromised both sides.

Before breaking up, the Convention had passed a war tax which the Right regarded as excessive, and which the Left condemned because it was not graduated. The Directory proposed replacing it with a compulsory loan and agreed to graduation. After the Five Hundred had relaxed the stringency of their directions, the Ancients adopted the resolution on 19 Frimaire, Year IV (December 10, 1795). The loan was demanded from the most heavily taxed quarter of the country's taxpayers, whom the central administration of the department had to divide into sixteen classes according to the registers of taxes. A few weeks was sufficient to show that the desired result would not be obtained: the *assignat* was accepted at one per cent, whereas the market rate was three or four times less; payment had to be made within two months, but the mere drawing up of the registers took longer, and as soon as they appeared, there was such a chorus of recrimination that the Councils passed a rectifying law, so that everything had to be begun all over again. Finally, the hard-pressed Directory diverted part of the loan from its purpose: it distributed among its creditors about ninety million francs in *rescriptions* which enabled them to obtain the yield of the loan from the tax collectors, a measure which put back in circulation the *assignats* that the Directory had taken out. Altogether, it obtained twenty-seven billion francs in paper money and twelve million francs in metallic currency. One can judge the extent of the sacrifice imposed on the bourgeoisie and the resentment that it inspired in that class from the fact that the Puy-de-Dôme, which had paid up 250,000 livres in face value at the time of the compulsory loan of 1793, had to pay two million in real value this time. Yet before the Directory had collected anything, it was obliged to recognize that the effort would be in vain: the *assignat* was no longer worth the paper it was printed on. On 30 Pluviôse (February 19, 1796), the issue came to a stop: the amount in circulation was estimated at thirty-nine billion.

Was it intended to revert in this way to metallic currency? In that case, the *assignats* which the loan had not absorbed had to be called in first of all. Eschassériaux had proposed exchanging them for "mortgage debentures," in other words bonds on national property which could not be paid for with anything else. But in the Ançients, Lebrun and Lecoulteux objected that the monetary and financial problem would remain. The metallic currency which had reappeared was put at no higher than 300 million, whereas at the end of the *ancien régime*, it had been estimated at over two billion; once the *assignat* had been withdrawn, the economy, deprived of currency and consequently of credit, would be mortally stricken. Then again, what would taxes be paid with? And where would the government find the money to finance the spring campaign? These arguments prepared the way for the bankers. One of them, Laffon-Ladébat, proposed in fact that they create an issuing house. As well as the bank notes which would guarantee its capital, it would print others, in return for the cession by the State of 1,200 million francs of national property, half in order to redeem the *assignats*, half in order to supply the Treasury. Perregaux, Fulchiron, and Récamier, who were among the founders of the Bank of France, were prepared to join in this arrangement. What they wanted was a super-bank which they would control and which, rediscounting the bills their clients would bring them, would give their business an unlimited extension. The Directory was in agreement. But the Left resisted. Robert Lindet, on behalf of the Jacobins, conducted a violent campaign in the *Ami des lois* against the subjection into which the Republic was going to be forced. On 3 Ventôse (February 22), in the Five Hundred, the project fell through. If a new paper money was indispensable, the majority wanted to issue it itself and this had to be accepted.

After Defermon had again proposed mortgage deben-tures which he called *mandats*, the Directory intervened to insist that they should be legal tender, and agreement was reached on the basis of this compromise. The law of 28 Ventôse, Year IV (March 18, 1796) created 2,400 mil-lion francs in *mandats territoriaux* which would be ac-cepted in payment of national property, to be handed over to any applicant on request and without auction. Six hundred million were to redeem the *assignats* and the rest was to go to the Treasury. The scheme raised such great hopes that the moratorium was annulled. For it to succeed, there would have had to be an immediate fiscal effort to balance the budget and restore confidence; measures would also have had to be taken to prevent a rise in prices by means of price control, and to prevent the collapse of foreign exchange by the control of imports and the obtaining of external credits. These conditions were excluded or unrealizable. Moreover, the *mandat* was discredited right from the start, because the *assignat* was accepted at the rate of thirty to one, whereas its real value was 400 to one at the very most. The catastrophe was overwhelming. At the beginning of April, the *mandat* of 100 francs was already worth only twenty; in July, it was no longer accepted in the commercial world. This time, thoroughly disillusioned, everybody accepted the need for a return to metallic currency. In Thermidor and Fructidor, the various taxes were declared payable in metallic currency or bills; on 1 Frumaire, Year V (November 21, 1796), the same condition was laid down for national property. Finally, on 16 Pluviôse (February 4, 1797), *assignats* and *mandats* ceased to be legal tender.

Public servants, rentiers and property owners had suffered a great deal; so had country landlords in many cases, although since Thermidor, Year III, half of farm rents had been payable in grain. The bourgeoisie, at least, had monopolized the greater part of what national property remained, although purchasers had been asked to pay a quarter of the agreed price in metallic currency, in violation of the contract. In the course of the winter, the workers had suffered even more, because their wages had been incapable of keeping up with the fantastic rise in prices. This rise had exceeded what the fall in the value of the *assignat* would have entailed: in December 1795, bread was selling in Paris at fifty francs a pound, or seven sous in metallic currency, whereas at the height of the food shortage of 1789 it had not exceeded four. The bargemen and stevedores in the ports, the best paid of all the workers, used to earn between six and nine livres, according to Lecoulteux, and now did not earn as much as 350.

To high prices was added a food shortage, because the peasants would no longer sell their produce except in return for metallic currency, and the harvest had been a poor one. On 7 Vendémiaire, Year IV (September 29, 1795), the Convention had confirmed the maintenance of controls, with the exception of maximum prices; grain could be sold only at a market, and a district could obtain it by means of requisitioning. But since the district administration had been abolished, the canton municipalities, which were composed of farmers and farm workers, put up a stubborn resistance to the towns which was scarcely weakened by the sending out of bailiffs. At the end of the winter, they stopped all supplies. The Directory helped the big cities by means of grain provided by the land tax, half of which was also payable in grain; they were supplied above all by foreign producers, for which the bourgeoisie furnished advance payments, thus increasing its influence still further. Moreover, at a time when the merits of freedom were widely lauded, circumstances made it necessary to enforce food controls much more strictly than in Year II.

In Paris, a great many people would have starved to death if the Directory had not continued the food distributions begun by the Committee of Public Safety, though limiting them to bread and meat. Theoretically, it provided one pound of bread a day in return for four sous in *assignats*, in other words for nothing, but the lack of money cut the ration to seventy-five grams; it was made up with rice, which it was impossible to cook, for there was a shortage of wood too. In Year IV, there was an increase of 10,000 deaths in the department of the Seine. Yet expenditure was enormous: nine million francs a day in December, 1795.

The general poverty maintained endemic agitation in the working class, which was perpetually trying to bring its wages up to the level of prices. Hostility to the rich was revived by the luxury which speculators, fops and *merveilleuses* flaunted impudently. The people's irritation turned against the Directory, against the men who had abolished the *maximum* and crushed the *sans-culottes* in Prairial; more and more frequently, people were heard to say that in Robespierre's time they had at least had bread to eat. This is what made the Jacobins a force to be reckoned with. Not content with thwarting the bankers' plans, they discussed at the Panthéon the restoration of the *maximum* and a ban on currency speculation. The Directory, on the other hand, was planning to abandon the poor to their fate and announce the suppression of food distributions except for the destitute. As in 1793, as in Prairial, the Jacobins could take advantage of a hunger riot.

The dates are conclusive. The food distributions were to stop on 1 Ventöse (February 21, 1796); feeling was so strong that they had to be continued. On the third, the plan for an issuing house was defeated. On the seventh, the Directory ordered the Jacobin Club to be closed, banning a few Royalist gatherings as well in order to save its face. The sentence was executed without a hitch the next day by General Bonaparte, who had been in command of the home army since Vendémiaire; hitherto he had made a great display of Jacobinism, but he had been asking for the army of Italy and was in fact given it on the twelfth. Having broken with the Jacobins, the Directory started dismissing their supporters and harrassing their papers. Outlawed once more, they resorted to conspiracy. The Thermidorian adventure began all over again.

This time, however, the activity of the Jacobins assumed a new appearance, because since January Babeuf's friends, especially Buonarroti, had obtained considerable influence in the Club, and in March Babeuf himself became the leader of the conspiracy. Now Babeuf, who was an even fiercer critic of civil equality than the Jacobins, and who considered political equality insufficiently effective, wanted to institute actual equality, with the result that the Jacobin plot is known as the Conspiracy of the Equals: he was a Communist, and with him Socialism, hitherto a utopian doctrine, became a political fact.

The son of a poor exciseman, married to an illiterate servant girl, Babeuf was well acquainted with the life of the poor. Becoming a Feudist, he had come in contact with the peasant community of Picardy where communal habits were still strong, as was the spirit of resistance to the big farmers with their ever-increasing power. Educated no one knows how, he had read a great deal, and as early as 1787 he had shown a certain sympathy for Communism and actual equality. So far this was only a theoretical preference and it was the Revolution which, by achieving civil equality, accelerated the progress of his thought; yet in 1791 he still considered it impossible to call for the agrarian law in public. The experiment of Year II took him further forward by showing him that the State could control the economy, and yet in Year III, he still hesitated to take direct action and confined himself to proposing to his friends the creation of a Communist association which would win over public opinion by its example. But in the course of the winter, exasperated by the terrible spectacle of poverty and by the treachery of Barras, Tallien, Fouché, and many others, forced by the Directory's persecution to go into hiding like Marat, and convinced by the failure of the compulsory loan and by the intrigues of the financial world that there was nothing to be hoped for from legal action, he came round to the idea of overthrowing the old world by violence.

Babeuf's Communism bore the mark of its time: it was aimed at distribution, not at production, the individualism of which had not yet been destroyed by capitalist concentration. The peasant would go on tilling his field, but as it would henceforth be the property of the nation, he would carry his harvest to the public warehouse. However, Babeuf differed sharply from previous Utopians, who had all been more or less inspired by moralizing and asceticism and who had envisaged little more than a rural community. It was to the self-interest of the proletariat—"its best guide" —that Babeuf appealed in order to awaken it to an idea of justice. He also counted on industry to spread abundance, and praised the machine which, in the service of the community, would lighten men's work; he pointed out that individual production was incapable of keeping pace with consumption. On the subject of consumption he was categorical: no trade or profession should receive preferential treatment; all stomachs were equal; Babeuf, in fact, was an *ouvriériste*, with no regard for the "intellectual." Nor was he a democrat in the political sense of the word; the Convention's recantations had inspired him with an incurable distrust of politicians, nor did he rely on the enslaved people whom it was in fact the revolution's task to set free. That revolution would be carried out by the dictatorship of the minority, instituted by violence. It is probably in this idea that Babeuf's historical importance lies: he arrived at a clear concept of that popular dictatorship of which Marat and the Hébertists had spoken without defining it; through Buonarroti, he bequeathed it to Blanqui and then to Lenin, who turned it into reality.

However, Babeuf's importance in the history of Socialism and his pre-eminent part in the Conspiracy of the Equals should not lead one to imagine that this conspiracy was fundamentally Communist in nature. Babeuf and his friends represented only a small minority of its members. The Panthéonists belonged to the bourgeoisie, and some of them, such as Amar and Le Peletier, were rich men; the subscribers to the *Tribun du peuple* belonged to the same class. The Jacobins' aim was political: they wanted to take their revenge on the Royalists and Thermidorians who had outlawed them, regain power and re-establish democracy. In all this, they were in agreement with Babeuf's supporters. But, once victory had been won, a break would have been inevitable and Babeuf would have been defeated. As for the proletariat, Communist propaganda did not have time to affect it and it remained indifferent.

It took a month for the plan for an insurrection to take shape. On 7 Germinal (March 27), Buonarroti was given yet another mission by the Directory to go and stir up a revolution in Piedmont. He did not leave Paris, for on the tenth Babeuf formed his Insurrectional Committee and Buonarroti joined it, together with Darthé and Le Peletier who were pure Jacobins, while others grouped around members of the Convention—Drouet, Amar and Lindet—still remained on one side. The Committee appointed an agent for each of the twelve arrondissements in Paris to direct its propaganda, which suddenly became very active in the form of pamphlets, posters, songs, and demonstrations. Military agents were also appointed to undermine the loyalty of the garrison, and especially of the Police Legion, which had been created after the *journées* of Prairial.

Circumstances remained favorable for the agitators. On 5 Germinal (March 25), the Directory, while continuing food distributions, raised the price of the ration considerably; on the fifteenth (April 4), rents became payable in *mandats*, but as mass expulsions would have followed on quarter-day, the Directory was obliged to make an exception of verbal leases which remained payable in *assignats*. La Revellière was terrified. Reubell hesitated to give the signal for repression, dreading a new White Terror; Barras tried to calm Babeuf and his supporters. It was Carnot who took the matter in hand, and from then on he persecuted the Jacobins with a somber fury. This volte-face surprised everybody. The reason for it is probably that Carnot had never ceased to be a conservative bourgeois who had rallied to the Mountain to finish with the counter-revolution and also out of ambition, but who had never approved of the social policy of Year II. But it is also that he had a despotic character which was infuriated by opposition: he outlawed the Jacobins of Year IV as he had helped to outlaw Hébert, Danton and Robespierre. At his suggestion, the Ministry of Police, taken from Merlin who returned to the Ministry of Justice, was entrusted to Cochon. On 27 Germinal (April 16), the Councils decreed the death penalty for anyone trying to bring about the restoration of the Monarchy or a return to the Constitution of 1793. Against the press, the Directory obtained, on the twenty-eighth, only an anodyne measure—the obligation that the printer give his name at the end of each publication—but the law passed the day before made it possible to prosecute journalists. Troops started circulating in Paris to break up crowds. The Police Legion having fallen under suspicion, it was decided to send it to join the armies, whereupon it mutinied on 9 Floréal (April 28).

The Babouvists decided to take advantage of the opportunity offered. On the 11th, the Committee summoned its agents and appealed to the members of the Convention. The measures to be taken to obtain power caused no difficulty, nor did those to be adopted afterwards; there was nothing Communist about them, and they resembled those of Year II. But Babeuf wanted to entrust the government to the Insurrectional Committee, admittedly attaching an assembly to it, but one elected by the rebels on the Committee's advice. The members of the Convention adhered to the principle of representative democracy and wanted to recall the Convention; the most they could obtain was to be incorporated in the assembly. The two sides did not come to an agreement until 18 Floréal (May 7). What would have come of this enterprise? Nothing but a new Prairial. The Directory had an even firmer grip on the reins of power than had the Committee of Public Safety. For the Jacobins, this was the worst mistake they could have made.

What is more, they had delayed too long; The Police Legion was dissolved on 11 Floréal without any serious incidents. They had been betrayed too: Grisel, one of the military agents, had sold his friends to Carnot. Babeuf was arrested on the twenty-first (May 10), as were Buonarroti and Drouet; all the Committee's papers fell into the hands of the Police, and the Directory issued 245 warrants for the arrest of the persons who were mentioned in those papers, often unknown to themselves. Although there had been no disturbance of the peace, the country's rulers were still in the grip of fear, and by railing against their prisoners, with the help of the papers, they terrified the bourgeoisie. All the more so in that in Prairial the monetary and economic crisis roused the workers once again; the Directory obtained authority to call up another 10,000 men.

All the same, the prosecution made only slow progress. Barras would have liked to reduce it to the minimum, and part of the Left, under the influence of Sieyès, refused to support the Directory. They were afraid of a new White Terror and the advantage which division among the Republicans would give to the Royalists. Carnot would have done honor to his own character if he too had shown some regret and reluctance to outlaw those who had previously fought by his side for the Republic. It was he, on the contrary, who adopted an inflexible attitude, and the majority of the Directorials joined with the Right to support him. But Drouet was a representative of the people, and the detailed procedure laid down for such an eventuality had to be observed; then again, the High Court existed only on paper and had to be organized. It was only during the night of 9-10 Fructidor (August 26-27), that the accused were taken in iron cages to Vendôme, where the High Court had been summoned. Drouet was not among them; he had just succeeded in escaping.

Up to the last minute, the Directory had been afraid that an attempt would be made to release them, and it was true that certain Jacobins had not given up the idea of direct action; they remained in communication with confederates in the army, and during the night of 23-24 Fructidor (September 9-10), they presented themselves at the Grenelle camp and called on the troops to fraternize. Once again they had been betrayed; Carnot was fully informed and this time had refrained from taking preventive action in order to have the opportunity of carrying out a bloody repression. The Jacobins, charged by the cavalry, left some dead behind; a great many of them were arrested and the Councils authorized domiciliary visits to search for the others. In order to have punishment meted out quickly, the Directory proposed that the prisoners be handed over to a military commission. It is true that there were a few soldiers among them, but a law of 22 Messidor (July 10) had just reserved for ordinary justice any trial in which civilians were involved; the law of 30 Prairial, Year III, which was cited as a precedent, was specifically concerned with the Vendeans and the Chouans. However, the Councils went ahead notwithstanding. The Directory even wanted to allow the accused only one barrister for them all; it did not get its way in this. The Military Commission of the Temple had thirty of the accused shot, including three former members of the Convention. Subsequently the proceedings were declared illegal by the Court of Appeal, on appeal by those sentenced to other penalties.

As for the Vendôme trial, it did not begin until the end of February, 1797, and lasted three months. Darthé withdrew into haughty silence, while Babeuf, less stoical in his attitude, pleaded that his writings had not been followed by a single act. The rest of the accused stood up to the judges and indulged in stormy demonstrations. The jury acquitted them all of the accusation of conspiracy. But the judges, illegally altering the indictment, called for the enforcement of the law of 27 Germinal and obtained an affirmative verdict for some of the accused. Darthé and Babeuf, sentenced to death, tried to commit suicide and were carried bleeding to the scaffold on 8 Prairial (May 27, 1797). Others remained in prison until the Consulate. They were not the only victims. A schoolteacher of the department of the Ain was guillotined under the law of 27 Germinal, as a supporter of the agrarian law.

The consequences of the new White Terror had appeared by the summer of Year IV. The juries acquitted the Vendémiairists, and one of them, the deputy Vaublanc, had been allowed to take his seat. In the theaters, patriotic songs had been abandoned. Benjamin Constant, whom Madame de Staël had pushed into politics, was recommending in his writings the formation of a great conservative party under the protection of the Directory. The Feuillants were received at the Tuileries and even dined there. Carnot considered that his triumph was complete and scribbled angry notes on the letters which his friend Garrau, a former member of the Convention, sent him from Italy to put him on his guard.

As Benjamin Constant had pointed out, this new trend implied concessions to the Right. The Directory, pressing on with the purge, dismissed all those whom the reactionaries denounced to it and replaced them with their candidates. In Provence in particular, radical changes were carried out. Fréron was recalled, the communal elections of Marseilles annulled, and the municipality appointed by the Directory; with a view to putting an end to civil war, the town was placed under martial law, but the command of the military division was given to the Royalist Willot, so that the White Terror could rage without let or hindrance. In the Councils, the Right asked at one and the same time for restrictions on the amnesty of 4 Brumaire and the repeal of the law of 3 Brumaire. There were confused debates for over three months. The new majority persisted in its onslaught on the Jacobins, but the old majority formed up again to uphold the law of 3 Brumaire. Finally, for the sake of peace and quiet, it was agreed to keep it as well as the amnesty, but extending exclusion from public office to those who had benefited from the amnesty. The law was passed on 14 Frimaire, Year V (December 10, 1796). However limited the success obtained by the Right was, it was nonetheless a harsh blow for the Jacobins at the approach of the elections. Carnot would have liked a reconciliation between the Republic and the Church to speed up the political compromise, and for a moment this seemed a possibility. Bonaparte was conquering Italy and had granted the Pope an armistice: at the end of July, Count Pierachi came, on behalf of Pius VI, to negotiate a peace with the Directory, at the very moment when the latter was deciding to make no attempt to destroy the Papal States. But it insisted that Pius VI revoke all his decisions on French affairs since 1789. This was asking the impossible; on the other hand, a *de facto* agreement was realizable, for Pierachi had with him a bull *Pastoralis sollicitudo*, calling upon the clergy to recognize the government of the Republic; but Pierachi kept it to himself, probably in the hope of obtaining in advance a few free concessions from the Directory. He was expelled and the negotiations broken off. The bull was handed over in any case to the Directory, which published it; the result was a tremendous controversy, the Royalist priests asserting that it was a forgery and declaring that even if it was genuine they would not obey, while the *soumissionaires* exulted.

43

The Right did at least obtain the repeal, under the aforementioned law of 14 Frimaire, Year V, of the article in
the law of 3 Brumaire, Year IV, which ordered the enforcement of the repressive measures of 1792 and 1793 against
the priesthood. It remained to be seen whether these
measures themselves were repealed at the same time. The
Republican administrations denied that this was the case,
and, for example, kept those priests who had been sentenced to reclusion in prison. In practice, however, the
clergy were treated gently. Cochon recommended the Directory's commissioners not to trouble quiet priests with
oaths and declarations, at least for the moment.

Control of public worship was abandoned with all the
more reason. In an article published on 6 Messidor, Year V
(June 24, 1797), the *Annales de la religion* would report that, out of the 40,000 parishes of old, nearly all had
revived public worship. Since the clergy's influence was
bound to be exerted in favor of the Right in most cases,
this was of great importance at the approach of the elections. The same was true of the repatriated émigrés, whose
numbers continued to grow. The sale of national property
slowed down at the same time. On several occasions, the
Left complained that people who had submitted tenders
had been unable to obtain their contracts. Finally, on 21
Pluviôse, Year V (February 8, 1797), Lamarque explained
that Ramel had given orders to this effect under a host of
pretexts which he could not judge, since only the Legislature could grant exceptions. This was neither more nor
less than the truth.

La Revellière's anticlericalism was finally aroused, and
this drew him nearer to Reubell and Barras. Starting in
Brumaire, the Directory forwarded to the Councils thou-

sands of documents reporting the violation of the laws on religious worship and the anti-Republican activities of the clergy. On 15 Pluviôse (February 3, 1797), the Directors signed the famous letter to Bonaparte in which they declared that the "Roman religion" would always be the "irreconcilable enemy of the Republic," and that it was therefore desirable "to destroy the center of the Roman Church," in other words "the papal government." Bonaparte took no notice and signed the Peace of Tolentino, but the "triumvirate" had nonetheless condemned the policy adopted towards the Papacy the previous July.

Since the beginning of the winter, the Right had had another reason for discontent. Peace had seemed close for a moment. Negotiations with the English had taken place at Lille, and, since the invasion of Germany had failed, Carnot had succeeded in having overtures made to Austria; in foreign policy too, he was now following the Right. These hopes had been disappointed, and in January, 1797, the victory of Rivoli gave reason to suppose that the spring campaign would make the Republic's triumph complete.

Moreover, the relations between the majority and the Directory gradually became strained. The Right took the attack onto ground where the Left, for its part, had its own reasons for opposition. Once again, the Directory had complained of the excesses of the press, and it seemed as if the deputies were going to give it satisfaction, for on both sides they made similar complaints about the opposing papers. However, when Daunou put forward three motions on peddling, the repression of slander and the founding of an official paper, the last two motions were rejected after protracted debates. The Right, which controlled most of the papers, did not want to interfere with them on the eve of the elections; the Left was upset when it was reminded that freedom of the press was the bastion of its opponents; both sides were worried about the increased authority which Daunou wished to confer on the Directory. The Councils' jealousy of the latter was revealed once more in connection with the reform of the gendarmerie. They passed this measure only after depriving the Directory of the choice of some of the officers; similarly, they refused to set up an agency for direct taxation, which would have removed the responsibility for the latter from the local authorities and transferred it to officials chosen by the government.

These were some of the symptoms of the crisis which the elections were going to provoke. Another sign of that crisis was the activity of the Royalists, which was increasingly obvious and seditious. It was not without reason that the "triumvirs" took fright. It was too late. The persecution of the Jacobins had opened the way for the revenge of Vendémiaire, all the more so in that the financial situation, which was appalling, made it easier by turning everybody against the government.

CHAPTER FOUR

The Finances of the Directory

It is much more difficult to return to metallic currency than to abandon it. The Directory found this out to its cost, and it owes a good deal of its unfortunate reputation to the difficulties of the operation.

The collapse of the *mandat* had led to another general moratorium. All contracts had once more been called in question, and until the end of the Directory, law after law was passed in attempts to reconcile as far as possible the contrary interests of creditors and debtors. This uncertainty was added to that which resulted from the laws on the émigrés and their relatives, and to that which surrounded the fate of the national estates, to discourage the spirit of enterprise and irritate public opinion.

Then again, the country areas were extremely disturbed. The food shortage had cruelly affected the peasants who did not harvest enough to live on—that is to say, the great majority—and with all the more reason the day laborers. As always happened in such cases, the number of beggars and tramps had increased and many of them had taken to brigandage. This evil had become far worse during the course of Year IV; bands of *chauffeurs*—who roasted their victims over fires in order to force them to give up their money—ravaged many regions. It was not very easy to distinguish between them and those who looted and killed in the name of the King and religion. On 27 Floréal, Year IV (May 16, 1796), the Directory ordered flying columns to be formed from the National Guard to attack both sorts, and on 15 Germinal, Year V (April 15, 1797), the Councils laid down the death penalty for brigands. But the evil, fostered by the economic crisis and the resulting unemployment, was to continue through the Consulate up to the time of the Empire.

If the crisis was prolonged, the reason once again was of a monetary nature. Metallic currency reappeared only very slowly, and never regained the volume of circulation that it had reached at the end of the *ancien régime*. After inflation, therefore, came deflation: prices fell sharply, all the more so in that the harvest of 1796 was excellent. This was good for the maintenance of law and order; the workers who remained in employment defended their wages with some success and the fall in food prices made life less difficult for them. But a fall in prices discourages production, and it had this effect until the end of the Directory.

These were all deplorable circumstances for a government which had to reorganize its finances, at a time when the continuing war was already making its task extraordinarily difficult. In Thermidor, Year IV, it had outlined the program which was called for to the Councils, discovering the extent of ordinary expenditure and war expenditure, making sure that the normal budget was balanced by means of taxation, and financing the war effort by means of exceptional financial measures. La Revellière, in his memoirs, stresses the efforts the Directory made to persuade the Councils to take action, and expresses justifiable indignation that it should have been ignored. Either the Five Hundred referred the *messages* to commissions which would never mention them again, or else those commissions eventually produced fragmentary plans which were endlessly debated; and, when some result was achieved, the Ancients often called the whole matter in question again. The debates revealed an ignorance which was surprising and doubtless sometimes spurious. The Councils expressed indignation, after having voted the sums asked for, at being told that the troops had not received their pay, that the government officials had not been paid, and that the hospitals were in a state of complete destitution. It was pointed out to them that it was not enough to vote sums for the Treasury to be able to find the money, and that the taxes themselves could not provide it if they were not voted in time. It was all in vain. This incapacity was linked with political motives: the Right made no secret of its hope of forcing the Directory to make peace for lack of money; the Left alleged that the Ministers did not provide accounts—which was true—and out of jealousy of the Executive did not scruple to hinder its activities; both sides pandered to the electors or to some interested group.

Nobody ever knew exactly how much the country's ordinary expenditure amounted to because the estimates of the various Ministries were passed by fits and starts throughout the year, a practice which made it possible to dispute the size of a deficit or even to maintain, as did Gibert-Desmolières, that there was a surplus. Then again, the taxes were voted belatedly: the land tax for Year V was voted on 18 Prairial (June 6) and the *mobilière*, which had been completely overhauled, only on 14 Thermidor (August 2), when the year was nearing its end. The drawing up of the registers—which was intrusted to municipal councilors who were in no hurry to pay, were often hostile and even more often incapable—aggravated delay. Until Year V, payment of the land tax was complicated by the obligation to pay half in grain, unless it could be proved that the harvest had not exceeded consumption. The tax collectors, appointed by the municipalities, were reluctant to exert pressure on the taxpayers in the midst of universal poverty; they themselves kept what they had received as long as possible in order to obtain interest from it. The Directory proposed setting up in each department an Agency of Direct Taxation composed of government officials, but without success, as has been seen. It did, however arrange that, for the time being, the registers should be copied from those used the year before; that payment should be made in installments; that the property of tax collectors should be treated as a surety for the collection of the taxes; and that they should be given authority to send bailiffs to the houses of recalcitrant taxpayers. But these means of enforcement were not applied until the eighteenth of Fructidor. In spite of everything, the results were not as contemptible as has been said. At the beginning of Year V, for example, the Puy-de-Dôme had paid ninety-three per cent of the land tax of Year III and seventy-two per cent of that of Year IV; however, the *mobilière* was much more in arrears, because right from the start it had oppressed the peasant to the benefit of the bourgeoisie.

Under the *ancien régime* the direct taxes were also paid belatedly, but the indirect taxes insured a daily revenue. This is why the Directory insisted that they be re-established, especially since the direct taxes did not provide enough money. The stamp duty was increased; the Five Hundred agreed to raise the duty on imported tobacco, to create a monopoly in powder and saltpeter, and to tax the salt mines; but the Ancients rejected all these measures. A toll was instituted for the upkeep of highways, but without any result, because the law which was to fix the amount was not passed. Only a tax on salt would have been really effective, but hardly anybody wanted it, either the Right or the Left, and it must be admitted that the country would not have tolerated the re-establishment of the *gabelle:* Napoleon himself would wait a long time before venturing to reimpose it. As for the country's extraordinary expenditure, only imaginary estimates of it were ever made. In order to meet it, the most important source of income was the sale of national property. On 18 Fructidor, Year IV (September 4, 1796), the property which came from the Belgium monasteries was put on sale, and a law of 16 Brumaire, Year V (November 6) re-established auction sales. In two years, the sales figures rose to 200 million francs, but the part payable in metallic currency or bills did not exceed three-eighths of the estimate; for the rest, "dead bills" were accepted, in other words, requisition bonds and deeds of outstanding debts, which produced no money.

The Directory was consequently still hard-pressed. No government, in a period of deflation, could have obtained enough money from the country through normal channels to pay off arrears and finance a war. What was needed was a controlled economy, a loan, or paper money, until the problem could be solved by the exploitation of conquered countries. A controlled economy was out of the question, and a loan was impossible, but people went on thinking about paper money; and indeed a moderate issue would have been all the more reasonable in that it would have stimulated the economy. In Frimaire, Year V, Ramel brought together some merchants from the principal commercial centers and some Parisian bankers; they refused to found a national bank as long as the political crisis had not been solved. This was a declaration of war by the businessmen of France upon the Directory. Other channels were explored. On 11 Nivôse (December 31, 1796), Réal, in a report on the Mortgage Code, made it possible for landowners to "liberate" their property by creating *cédules* which were transferable by endorsement. The motive behind this measure is obvious: it would have been possible to impose on landowners a compulsory loan payable in *cédules*, which would have become a new currency. Jourdan (of the Bouches-du-Rhône), one of the leaders of the Right, denounced the idea in an impassioned speech, and the proposal was rejected. On 9 Germinal (March 29), the Directory put on sale a certain number of Parisian properties which could be purchased exclusively in *rente* certificates, under the pretext of amortizing the

debt; in reality, if the attempt had succeeded, these certificates would have become a currency and they could have
been increased in number to pay for national property.
Once again, Jourdan stepped into the breach, declaring
that he did not want the Directory to be given this means
of prolonging the war indefinitely; going further, he recalled
that the Great Book mixed up legitimate rentiers with
contractors whose usurious debts had been paid in *rente*
certificates, and he called for a revision of the National
Debt. The sale of the Parisian property was approved, but
the Directory left it at that. In these circumstances, there
was nothing left for it but to imitate the King who, in similar cases, used to resort to expedients known as "extraordinary affairs." This is what it did.

It rejected the idea of a controlled economy, but it retained requisitioning without any law authorizing it to do
so. It had scarcely been installed in power before it had
ordered the use of requisitioning; the system provided it
with grain and fodder, horses and cattle, not to mention
wagons and their drivers; price control was not restored,
but payment was made in vouchers which the government
took back in acquittance of taxes or in return for national
property. This was not enough, and, as the Thermidorians
had done, the Directory turned for help to the financiers
who, alone, had enabled the *ancien régime* to wage its
wars. In the course of Year IV, the ministers placed contracts with the "commissaries," while the Treasury, in
order to obtain metallic currency or advances, came to an
understanding with the *faiseurs de services*, who were
also bankers and merchants. As far as the "commissaries"
were concerned, the Directory finally realized that an excessive number of contracts made supervision impossible

and, by putting the purchasers in competition with one another, fostered a rise in prices. On 3 Nivôse, Year V (December 23, 1796), it decided to entrust the provisioning of all the armies and the navy to a small number of specialized companies. In other words, it favored capitalist concentration, pleading too that these companies, with greater funds at their disposal, would provide better service, and, buying in bulk, would cut down expenses. But in the existing state of the economy, there were no financiers sufficiently powerful to take on such responsibilities and the undertaking had to be subdivided much more than had been hoped.

The contractors paid in advance; this was indeed their *raison d'être*. Yet they themselves had to be paid in the end. As a result, as long as inflation continued, they frequently abandoned their responsibilities, being unable to carry them out with the assignats and *mandats* which were given them at par. Although constantly condemned, the executive agencies of Year II therefore remained in existence for a long time, since these deficiencies had to be provided for. After the return to metallic currency, the difficulties were of a different sort, but the general situation was not much improved.

As early as 1795, shortage of money had obliged the Directory to establish an order of payment: three times a month, on the advice of the Ministers, it made a note of the most urgent debts and distributed the funds which it hoped to have at its disposal during the next ten days. In October, 1796, the Councils legalized this expedient, on the understanding that the armies and the navy would have preference; the Directory added that until further notice no account would be taken of arrears. This did not mean,

54

however, that the favored contractors were out of trouble, because, as far as the contents of the Treasury were concerned, the Directory was in the same position as the *ancien régime*. In Paris, the revolution had brought about the unity of the Treasury, but its bookkeeping was so involved that it was incapable of presenting a financial statement or of rendering accounts. The provincial tax collectors were not kept under close supervision, and moreover communications were too slow for the Treasury to be informed every ten days about their returns. The Ministers gave the contractors warrants for payment to be redeemed by the Treasury, and Ramel gave them *rescriptions* or bonds to be redeemed by the tax collectors. But when these warrants and bonds were presented, the coffers were often empty, or alleged to be empty. The government would then help the contractors to the best of its ability. Assets belonging to the Republic were lodged with them as security, and they pledged them to obtain credit; the Regent, the most famous of the crown diamonds, was thus entrusted to Treskov, a Prussian merchant who supplied horses, and deposited as security in the Bank of Berlin. Much use was made of the Batavian *rescriptions*, bonds provided by Holland to cover what was still due of the war indemnity inscribed in the Treaty of The Hague, which was to be paid in annual installments in accordance with an agreement of 1796. Accommodation bills, the so-called *cavalerie*, which were in constant use in the commercial world of that day, were also employed. In every case, the Treasury undertook to provide for the bills when they fell due, even if it had to begin again. Sometimes, authority was given for the raw materials or articles which the creditor could use to be removed from the State warehouses.

The contractors began to grow weary of all this. That is why the law of 16 Brumaire, Year V, authorized the acceptance of ministerial warrants in payment for national property. Paulée, for example, acquired over 600 hectares in the department of the Nord, and was authorized to buy property to the value of sixteen million francs in Belgium. All the same, at the beginning of 1797 the Five Hundred were informed that the contractors refused to continue their services unless they were given effective guarantees. As a result, the Councils authorized the so-called *délégations:* The Directory surrendered to its creditors specific parts of the Republic's receipts, notably cuttings in the national forests or the yield of taxes in certain specified departments, thus re-establishing the much-criticized *anticipations* of the *ancien régime,* which the Constituent Assembly had forbidden. Even so, the security was never satisfactory, since the yield of a tax remained problematical. In many cases, the creditor was forced to ask for a fresh assignation, and, as a paradoxical consequence, he would not hesitate, in order to obtain the assignation which struck him as the best, to pay the Treasury a certain amount of cash.

Irregularly paid and never sure of being paid at all, the contractors covered themselves by raising their prices. The Directory never tired of telling the Councils that things would go on like this until they provided for the replenishment of the Treasury. Nor was this all; the contractors pleaded that they had no option but to hold the State for ransom because they themselves were held for ransom by the State's own agents: the Treasury employees and the tax collectors demanded a commission before paying them; the war commissioners and the warehousemen refused to sign receipts when deliveries were made, except on the same condition. The contractors were therefore not all swindlers, in spite of current opinion, but they were businessmen: they took advantage of the situation to increase their profits when they could. Nor is there any doubt that many of them did not scruple to resort to illegal intrigues. While complaining about the Republic's agents, they were the first to bribe them in order to get their fraudulent deliveries accepted; similarly, they did not hesitate to tempt politicians or to win over those who approached them in order to obtain leonine contracts.

Under every form of government, monetary and financial disorder engenders corruption, and it is in order to praise Bonaparte—who, however, did not succeed in putting a stop to it—that such corruption has been depicted as the Directory's exclusive privilege; but it cannot be denied that the political world exposed itself to suspicion at that time, and that in several cases the suspicion was justified. The Directory and the Ministers were largely responsible for this state of affairs: contracts were not allocated in public to the lowest tenderer, but in the secrecy of government offices; with the *faiseurs de services* who provided currency, foreign bills or advances, it was indeed impossible to deal in any other way; then again, the decadal order of payments gave the government a despotic power of discrimination among creditors, and the same could be said of the delivery of assignations by means of *rescriptions*, and of the *délégations*. The politicians were no less exposed to suspicion. Some made fortunes, legally no doubt, but to the indignation of the public; Lozeau, for example, by speculating in salt; Rovère, Le Paige and Abolin by dealing in national property; and Gérard by financing the Tivoli Gardens and Ruggieri's firework displays. How could anyone fail to think that they might well use their positions to help their interests and sell their support to businessmen? In the provinces, the members of the local administrations and the Directory's commissioners were similarly suspect. There is no doubt, for example, that Tallien and Fouché, Barras and Talleyrand made money out of everything. Barras was openly associated with Ouvrard, the biggest speculator of the age and general contractor to the Navy, to whom he passed Madame Tallien when she started costing him too much; and when Talleyrand learned that he was a Minister, his first reaction was to exclaim: "I must make a huge fortune!"

A host of scandals, big and small, revealed the evil. The most famous concerned the Flachat Company and the Dijon Company. The former supplied the Army of Italy. Unable to secure payment, it obtained the revenue of the war taxes, as well as the proceeds of the sale of the English merchandise seized at Leghorn. Bonaparte maintained friendly relations with it at first, but it did not trouble to redeem his orders for payment, and it was not long before he denounced its malpractices. The Directory ended up by summoning its directors before a court-martial; they challenged the competence of the court, then escaped. Now it so happened that one of Flachat's partners was Laporte, a former member of the Convention and a friend of Reubell's; it is easy to guess what inference the public drew. The case of the Dijon Company, which served as a cover for the financier Hinguerlot, compromised Ramel and the Treasury. He had been instructed to speculate for a fall in the *mandats* to justify their demonetization. When the operation had to be liquidated, the government joined issue with the company; there followed a prolonged lawsuit, which the company won, as well as stormy debates in the Councils. There can be no doubt about Hinguerlot's fraudulent maneuvers, but the fact remains that the government had conspired to debase its own currency and that the swindler had obtained help from some unexpected sources.

Quite apart from the discredit which the shortage of money, by its demoralizing repercussions, cast on the Directory, it directly compromised it in the eyes of the electoral body by harming private individuals, already seriously affected by the monetary crisis. The peasants, paid in requisition bonds, were forced to sell them cheap in order to obtain funds. The rentiers were in an even worse plight: the Directory had dared to promise them only a quarter of the face value of their dividend coupon in metallic currency, but it was unable to find even that; they were accordingly given "quarter bonds," payable in metallic currency when the Republic could manage it, and "three-quarter bonds" which could be used for nothing but the payment of taxes or the purchase of national property. In order to live, they had to sell them to the first speculator they met.

Then again, the whole country suffered from the dilapidation of the public services. The government officials were paid only at irregular intervals; the gendarmes sold their horses, which they could not afford to feed, at a time when brigands were scouring the country; the roads fell into disrepair. To relieve the budget, the cost of the courts, the central schools and public assistance had been transferred to the local administrations; they met this cost only by means of a special rate, which was limited and inadequate, and which was as slow to come in as the taxes.

The taxpayers showed no great eagerness to fulfill their obligations; they nonetheless lent a ready ear to the Royalist opposition which imputed to war, waste and corruption, in other words to the Directory, all the evils of which the financial crisis, so complex in its origins, was the inexhaustible source.

CHAPTER FIVE

The Elections of Year V; the Conflict Between the Directory and the Councils

The anti-Jacobin repression and Bonaparte's victories, by consolidating the Directory, had favored reconciliation with the Republic to such an extent that the King's representatives—the Paris Agency, directed by the Abbé Brottier—thought fit to make advances to the Constitutionalists, some of whom, it was said, were thinking of the Duc d'Orléans. The link was arranged by Dandré, a former Counselor to the High Court of Provence and an influential member of the Constituent Assembly, who was a supporter of legal action. The Agency recommended meeting its interlocutor's wishes, but Louis XVIII—who, obliged to leave Verona, had ended up by finding refuge with the Duke of Brunswick at Blankenburg—remained intractable. All the same, it did not escape him that the election of a right-wing majority would open favorable prospects for him; without giving up the idea of using force, he approved the making of plans to fight the elections.

The activity of the Royalists therefore took on an increasingly ambiguous character, with the Absolutists and Constitutionalists, Chouans and politicians acting together, while retaining their preferences and mental reservations. In the summer of 1796, the Paris Agency had founded an association called the "Friends of Order," which was supposed to unite all the Directory's opponents in the constitutional sphere, and inside which a smaller group of "Legitimate Sons" was to be recruited, whose members would be initiated in the plans for a Restoration and in the preparation of an insurrection. Dandré, who also wanted to found an association to fight the elections, adopted the Friends of Order, which came out into the open under the name of the Philanthropic Institute, incidentally keeping as its leader Despomelles, a member of the Paris Agency. In the Sarthe, the Institute was organized by Rochecot, a Chouan. At Bordeaux, its leader was a creole, Dupont-Constant, but he was backed up by a committee dedicated to violent action. Moreover, Dandré remained in touch with the Swabian Agency, which was directed by Précy, who had been in command in Lyons in 1793, and which gave orders to the conspirators in the east and south. The funds were provided by Wickham, the English agent in Switzerland, with the approval of Grenville and Pitt. The English, while not discouraging the advocates of insurrections, considered that the Monarchy would only be restored in

France in a constitutional form, and this was also the opinion of the Genevese Mallet du Pan and Francis d'Ivernois, the leading publicists of the counterrevolution. It was with English money that Dandré organized a personal police force and postal service and founded newspapers, notably the *Mémorial*, to which La Harpe and Fontanes contributed. The Anglo-Royalist plot which the Directory denounced therefore existed in reality: only it must be remembered that many people played its game without knowing that they were doing so. It is important too not to exaggerate the size of the Royalist organization: the military resources at the conspirators' disposal remained very slight, and the Philanthropic Institute does not seem to have played a considerable part in the elections, having been formed so far in only a few departments. The reactionaries' success was due above all to the electors' lively discontent, whose complex causes have been mentioned already.

Moreover, it soon became obvious that unity of action was far from having been achieved. The King having criticized the Paris Agency's complaisance towards the Constitutionalists, it returned at an unfortunate time to a policy of conspiracy. One of the Royalists' hopes had always been to win over some general or other. They had unsuccessfully put out feelers towards Hoche, before trying to murder him; but in the Army of the Rhine and Moselle, Moreau was a friend of Pichegru's and it was Régnier, his chief of staff, whom Mathieu Dumas had approached to obtain a commander and recruits with the right ideas for the Guard of the Legislature. The Paris Agency approached this commander, General Ramel, and believed it had won him over, as well as Malo who was in command of a regiment of dragoons. However, they ended up by warning the Directory, and it was as well for them that they did so, for the Directory had already been informed by the Prince de Carency, the son of the Duc de la Vauguyon, who had only recently been a Minister for Louis XVIII. Brottier and his accomplices were arrested on 11 Pluviôse, Year V (January 30, 1797). They were charged only with enticement, so that they could be summoned before a court-martial; they challenged its competence and lodged an appeal. The military commission itself referred the matter to the Five Hundred, where there was a lively debate; but the Directory had forestalled this move by forbidding communication of the documents in the case to the Court of Appeal, whose jurisdiction did not extend to military law. The Five Hundred gave way. The judges, however, felt that they were being intimidated, for they convicted only four of the accused, and sentenced them only to imprisonment. But in the course of the preliminary examination, one of them, Duverne de Presle, had revealed everything he knew about the activities of the Royalists. The Directory kept his confession secret. It would publish it only on the eighteenth of Fructidor in order to denounce the Anglo-Royalist plot. In any case, the Paris Agency was promptly reconstituted under the name of the Royal Council, under the Duc de la Tremoille, assisted by the Abbé de Lamare.

The affair brought no benefit to the Directory; Royalist propaganda represented it as a police plot and went on as before. The priests, while operating in their own interests, were its most active auxiliaries. The local administrations, most of the time, helped it to the best of their ability by expurgating the electoral registers and by allowing the Republicans to be excluded from the primary assemblies. The

Directory reacted feebly. A decree denied the right to vote
to all who were inscribed on the list of émigrés, but a law
confirmed it for those who had been provisionally struck
off. The Councils were asked to impose on all electors the
oath of hatred for the Monarchy and the Constitution of
1793; they confined themselves to asking for a promise
which drew hilarious comment from the Royalist papers.
The number of voters was greater than in Year IV, but not
much greater, at least in the country districts: twenty-eight
per cent in the south. Barely a dozen departments retained
Republican representatives, and only eleven members of
the Convention survived, several of whom were Royalists.
Some elections were characteristic: Willot in Marseilles,
Imbert-Colomès in the Rhône. The department of the
Seine elected only Monarchists, including the Comte de
Fleurieu, the former tutor to the Dauphin. Pichegru had
been elected in the Jura, and Royer-Collard in the Marne.
The right-wing majority, now specifically Royalist, appeared
overwhelming.

The elections immediately had serious repercussions.
Bonaparte having signed the peace preliminaries shortly
afterwards, at Leoben, the Directory was obliged to ratify
them under pain of exasperating public opinion and irritat-
ing the general, whose support was seen as a possible means
to salvation. In the Five Hundred, the Right started to act
boldly: on 15 Floréal (May 4), it secured the repeal of the
law of 3 Brumaire, Year IV, although admittedly the
Ancients refused to confirm it. Inside the Directory, the
split became final. Reubell thought that the Directory
could take the left-wing majority in hand again by speaking
openly: he wanted to ask it to annul the elections and
adopt fresh exceptional measures, in other words carry out

the *coup d'état* which would take place on 18 Fructidor, but by parliamentary methods and without having recourse to the army. Carnot categorically opposed this suggestion; in his eyes the government's duty was to bow to the legally constituted majority. In the Five Hundred, somebody proposed that the Councils in office should institute a check on the powers of the newly elected members, an operation which would have made it possible to eliminate at least some of them; this device, which would be used in Year VI, was rejected this time.

The immediate question was who was to leave the Directory; if La Revellière, Reubell or Barras was indicated by the ballot, the majority would change sides. Reubell suggested insuring the election of a Republican by anticipating the expiration of the prescribed period by means of the resignation of one of the Directors whom the present Councils would have to replace, but this ingenious device assumed that the Five were in agreement. Couldn't the ballot be gerrymandered? This was what the Royalists feared, and the Right had a law passed which made it public. Chance saved the Republic: it was Letourneur who left.

Meeting on 1 Prairial (May 20), the Ancients elected Barbé-Marbois as their president, and the Five Hundred elected Pichegru as theirs. Acting together, they recalled the deputies who had been excluded under the law of 3 Brumaire, and then elected to the Directory Barthélemy, the Republic's representative in Switzerland, where he had negotiated the treaties of Basle. It was not a good choice; cold-shouldered by the triumvirs, and regarding Carnot as a scoundrel because he was a regicide, Barthélemy, who in any case had little talent, soon resigned himself to impotence. The majority was led by the Clichy Club, to which several hundred deputies belonged, and above all by a much smaller group which met at the house of Gibert-Desmolières. It soon became obvious that the majority was as complex as the interests and sentiments which had brought about its election. The "White Jacobins," as Thibaudeau called them, who wanted to set about restoring the Monarchy without delay, did not control it. They were outnumbered by the Constitutional Monarchists who distrusted them, and above all by those deputies collectively known as the Belly, who were chiefly inspired by hostility towards the members of the Convention, and who, though sympathetic to the Monarchy, preferred to devote their attention to improvements which were immediately realizable; both groups, shrinking from violence and the harm it would cause, envisaged a provisional agreement with the Directors which would make it possible to wait peacefully for the elections of Year VI. The conservative Directorials such as Thibaudeau and Doulcet were inclined to help them. If the "White Jacobins" had had a leader, they could probably have prepared a *coup d'état* without the majority daring to stop them; they counted on Pichegru, who still enjoyed considerable prestige in the army, his treason remaining unknown; but he was not the man they thought he was. Pleasure attracted him even more than power; he seems to have been ill at ease in this political world with which he was unfamiliar; he may have wondered whether the government had not got proof of his treason; and finally, he was not sure what his fate would be under a restoration. In short, until the eve of the eighteenth of Fructidor, he tended towards a policy of temporization. The impotence of the majority is reflected in the correspondence of Mallet du Pan, who refers scathingly to the violent individuals whose mad audacity may compromise everything, and despises the Constitutionalists who lack courage and are unwilling to take any risks. Who, then, could be relied on? The "Anglo-Royalist plot" confined itself to trivialities. The Left, moreover, stood up to it, and several times, especially in the Ancients, defeated its opponents or at least forced them to postpone their plans.

The attention of the Right was drawn first of all to the situation in Santo Domingo and the administration of Commissioner Santhonax, who was attacked with incredible violence. The misfortunes of the settlers were brought up and it was decided that they should be repatriated at the Republic's expense. In reality, the disagreement was about the slavery of the Blacks, and no attempt was made to conceal the fact, although nobody dared to call for the restoration of slavery. The Directory had softened the blow by spontaneously recalling its commissioners. As there could be no question of introducing constitutional government into the colonies, the moderates allowed themselves to be persuaded to authorize the government to send out new agents.

The law of 3 Brumaire, Year IV was then considered, and was repealed almost without discussion. The majority incidentally made a point of showing its impartiality by also repealing the disqualification which the law of 14 Frimaire, Year V had imposed on those who had been amnestied, and it refused to listen to the extremists who had once again suggested revoking the amnesty itself.

On the clergy and religious worship, discussion was more prolonged, and in a few respects the majority changed sides.

Right from the start, countless petitions had pleaded the cause of the priests and had inflamed passions. The Directory itself had suggested that the situation should be clarified: were the repressive laws of 1792 and 1793 abrogated or not? At the same time, on 28 Prairial (June 16) Camille Jordan had presented a report on the subject of freedom of worship; it was regarded as symbolic because it asked that the clergy should henceforth be dispensed from oath or promise, and that the ringing of bells should be authorized, thus earning the author the nickname of "Jordan-les-Cloches." At bottom, his proposals were very moderate, for he agreed to the confinement of religious worship to church premises and agreed to penalties against ecclesiastics who used religion as a political weapon. But he had been unable to refrain from inveighing against his opponents, and on 20 Messidor (July 8), General Jourdan retorted by evoking the memory of the Republicans who had fallen in the civil war stirred up by the priests, whereupon Lemerer added to the tumult by praising "the religion of our fathers." Finally, the laws of 1792 and 1793 were formally repealed on 26 Messidor (July 14). But Boulay de la Meurthe insisted that the declaration of submission to the laws should be maintained, and, in spite of the obvious partiality of the president Henry-Larivière, this was agreed to in principle, on the twenty-eighth, by 210 votes to 204. The Ancients postponed their approval of the repeal of the repressive laws until 7 Fructidor (August 24); in any case, the text of the declaration remained in the works, and the law of 7 Vendémiaire, Year IV had not yet been retouched when the *coup d'état* occurred. Fierce attacks by Gibert on secular education, which Bailleul defended, and others on

69

divorce, which Henry-Larivière condemned in the name of the Catholic Church, only served to make the atmosphere stormier and stormier.

For the émigrés, the results were not very effective either. A further stay of execution was granted to the Alsatians, with an extension of the amnesty to the nobles, but the Ancients rejected the resolution. They left in abeyance the one which had once again authorized the Toulon rebels to return to France, and yet another which dispensed the relatives of émigrés from all the laws directed against them. Agreement could be reached only on the émigrés whom a storm had shipwrecked on the coast near Calais, and who for two years had been sent from one court to another, none being able to bring itself to enforce the law which condemned them to death. It was decided that they should be re-embarked on a ship bound for a neutral country.

The relative impotence of the majority might have calmed the Republicans' fear if reaction had not been unleashed in the country. The administrations, now almost universally hand-in-glove with the Royalists, were systematically letting the Republican legislation fall into abeyance and reducing the commissioners to inactivity; the courts were displaying an obvious partiality; the Philanthropic Institute was multiplying its offshoots in most of the departments; nearly all the outlawed priests had openly reappeared; the émigrés were returning without let or hindrance; one and all were venting their fury on the purchasers of national property; violence was increasing even in Paris; in Provence, the Directory instructed Bonaparte to protect the Republicans, and he sent Lannes there with some troops from the Army of Italy.

To meet the growing danger, the Republicans tried to

regroup themselves. In Paris, a Constitutional Club met in Messidor, not at the Hôtel de Salm, as is usually said, but at the Hôtel de Montmorency, in the Faubourg Saint-Germain. Others were formed in Paris—about forty, it is said—and in the provinces, especially in the south where the need was particularly pressing. The Constitutional Club which had set the movement on foot had been created by Directorials; Benjamin Constant was the oracle of the Club, together with Sieyès and Talleyrand. But the Directory suspected, not without reason, that the Jacobins would come to the forefront in most of the others, and it was probably for this reason that it refrained from defending them when they were denounced on 24 Messidor (July 12) as preparing a demonstration for July 14: on 5 Thermidor (July 23), the clubs were closed, although they were authorized by the Constitution.

In all this, the Directory had shown itself as conciliatory or resigned. The Right drove it to extremes by trying to deprive it of the means of governing. It re-established co-optation in every case of a partial vacancy in the administrations; it gave orders for a complete change of personnel in the central offices of the big towns after each municipal election; it forbade the proclamation of marital law except in the case of investment by the enemy or by rebels. Above all, Gibert-Desmolières set out to deprive the government of the few resources that the financial crisis had left it.

He was guided by the Treasury, which had been a nest of counterrevolutionaries since the beginning of the Revolution; in constant conflict with the Directory, and threatened on account of its part in the Dijon Company affair, it was trying to re-ingratiate itself. In 21 Prairial (June 14), for two and a half hours, Gibert reeled off a report which recommended suppressing *anticipations*, rejecting ministers' warrants in payment for national property and consolidating them officially as Treasury scrip, entrusting the Treasury alone with purchases of metallic currency and bills and with all loans and pledges, and finally, conferring on it the power to endorse orders for payment and to divide the funds available among the various services as it thought fit, without preference for the armies or the navy. If these proposals were approved, the Directory would be deprived of all the expedients which had enabled it to govern somehow or other until now, and, most important of all, it would find it impossible to finance the war effort. Yet peace had not been concluded. It was in fact precisely to force the Directory to make peace at any price that the Right wanted to reduce it to impotence, and on 30 Prairial, it passed the articles concerning the powers of the Treasury. The Left protested indignantly; on 1 Messidor (June 19), in the Five Hundred, the tumult reached its highest pitch and deputies came to blows. However, Thibaudeau and his friends had also protested against the attack being made on the government's authority, and their arguments had created an impression; it was stipulated that the Treasury would have to give precedence to military expenditure. This reservation did not strike the Ancients as adequate; they rejected the resolution. This was a counter-thrust: Gibert's campaign continued, but its only result was to persuade the Directory to make an end of it all.

In the meantime, while undermining the government's authority, the reactionaries also tried to enter it by getting the Ministers changed in accordance with their wishes. Carnot joined Barthélemy in approving this method of insuring that the regime should become parliamentarian.

They tried in vain to detach La Revellière from Reubell, but Barras, it seems, gave his assent; it is even alleged that he was negotiating with the King's envoys. In fact, he was playing a double game. As soon as the Councils had assembled he sent one of his deputy friends, Fabre de l'Aude, to ask Bonaparte for his help if necessary; Fabre returned at the beginning of Messidor with an encouraging report and a document taken from the papers of Antraigues, a Royalist agent in the Tsar's pay who had just been arrested. This document was the account given him by Montgaillard, the Prince de Condé's agent, of his relations with Pichegru. Perhaps Barras was irritated at the discovery that he was not the only instrument of the Restoration. In any case, he immediately went into action, and, since Bonaparte was too far away, appealed to Hoche, who was now in command of the Army of the Sambre and Meuse. On 13 Messidor (July 1), the general dispatched some troops who were ostensibly supposed to be going to Brest to reinforce an army bound for Ireland, but who in fact made for Paris.

They were approaching the capital when, on the 26th, the Directors, of a common accord, proceeded to take a vote on the purging of the Ministries. To Carnot's disappointment, Barras voted invariably the same way as La Revellière and Reubell. The ministers dear to the Right —Bénézach, Cochon and Petiet—were dismissed. True, Delacroix and Truguet were also dismissed, but Ramel and above all Merlin, who was particularly detested by the Royalists, retained their positions. Among the new appointments, two caused a sensation. Talleyrand took over the Ministry of External Relations; Madame de Staël had introduced him to Barras, who had agreed to support him

—they were born to understand each other. The Ministry of War fell to Hoche, and the full meaning of this choice became apparent when Petiet informed the reactionaries of the approach of the troops. There could be no doubt about it: a *coup d'état* was imminent.

The intervention of the generals was in fact going to solve the crisis, bring the Republic back to a dictatorship, and at the same time place it at their mercy. But the regime was not the only thing at stake; the Republic's foreign policy was also involved, for Bonaparte was taking a stand against the Councils only in order to make himself arbiter of war and peace.

CHAPTER SIX

The Directory
and the Coalition

Thanks to the armies of the Revolutionary government, the Thermidorians had occupied Belgium, Holland, and the Left Bank of the Rhine. Prussia and Spain, abandoning the Coalition, had negotiated with them at Basle. But England and Austria remained in arms, and in 1795 the reverses suffered in the autumn campaign had brought the Germans back into Palatinate. The Thermidorians had been unable either to make peace or to wage war. In Year VIII, the same would be said of the Directory.

It was not impossible to defeat Austria, who could not count on receiving any effective help from her allies. True, the French armies were in a pitiful state: between October, 1794, and January, 1796, their strength fell from 750,000 men to 410,000, largely through desertion; however, by various shifts and devices, the Directory was able to send them into enemy country in the spring of 1796. Moreover, Austria too was in a bad way; if she gave in, England might one day end up by wearying of the fight; but there could be no hope of this unless there was a durable peace on the Continent, and that depended on the frontiers which the Republic wanted to obtain for France.

Only accomplices of foreign governments wanted to return to the frontiers of 1789; the advocates of the "former limits," such as Mathieu Dumas, usually suggested that they be improved: France should keep Avignon, Savoy, and part of the Netherlands. The Thermidorians had gone further: they had annexed Belgium. They maintained that this union with Belgium had been implicitly ratified by the plebiscite on the Constitution, and moreover that this Constitution forbade any dismemberment of the national territory. Of these two assertions, the first was debatable and the second false, for the ban applied only to secret treaties. However, the Directory adopted them as its own and steadfastly insisted that the "constitutional limits" were sacrosanct. As a result, the only question that remained was to know whether the French should advance to the country's "natural frontiers"—which, as matters stood, meant as far as the Rhine. The Thermidorians had confined themselves to keeping the future open by forcing Prussia to promise her eventual support for the cession of the left bank of the Rhine for the Empire. Opinions were far from being unanimous, even in the army: Kléber, for example, repudiated the French conquests, but the Royalists were

violently hostile to the natural frontiers policy, and as a
result the Republicans came to support it. This is what the
Directory did. Carnot, who had spoken in 1793 in support
of the natural frontiers and, more recently, of the union
with Belgium, had rallied to the "former limits" since he
had joined up with the Right; but Reubell, who was in control of foreign affairs, was the staunchest advocate of annexation, and his colleagues followed him. There was no
lack of reasons for disputing whether this decision was lawful and above all whether it was wise. The Thermidorians
had promised prosperity and liberty; peace was therefore
indispensable to them. The natural frontiers policy was
bound to make that peace more difficult and more fragile.

Was it at least compatible with a peace of some duration? It has been argued that it was, but without convinc-
ing proof. Austria was not insistent on retaining Belgium;
like Prussia, she was reluctant to give up the left bank of
the Rhine and thus compromise herself in the eyes of the
Germans, but both countries were ready to accept the situation if they could obtain some compensation. England,
since the reign of William of Orange, had made it a principle to prevent France from conquering the Netherlands,
but by herself she was incapable of taking them back from
her. True, if the English and the Germans gave way, that
did not mean that they would never return to the attack.
But that was not the question for the Directory; all they
wanted to know was whether the Republic had a chance of
obtaining recognition for the natural frontiers and of keeping them long enough to put herself in a position to defend
them successfully. There can be no doubt that the answer
was in the affirmative. But on two conditions: first of all
it was essential that Prussia should find compensation in

rounding off her frontiers in Germany, Austria in extending her territory in Italy, England in the undisputed domination of the seas and the acquisition of colonies; secondly it was essential that France should be satisfied with these frontiers and should not try to extend them.

These conditions were difficult to fulfill. When they had declared war, the Girondins had promised to liberate the oppressed peoples; La Revellière could not forget this, and the Italian and Swiss refugees still less; it was intolerable, they argued, that the Republic should return to the foreign policy of the *ancien régime* and come to terms with the "tyrants," allowing them to share out nations like cattle. Moreover, this hatred for the new France was constantly being revealed; the safety of the Republic depended on her dethroning them—if not in the whole world, at least in Europe. Every time that danger revived the revolutionary spirit, the elements it contained of national interest and romantic enthusiasm were reawakened too. Now, if France insisted on dominating Germany and Italy, it would be impossible to come to terms with Austria; before long the Coalition would re-form again, and the result would be perpetual war. Under the influence of Reubell, who was resolutely hostile to such a development, the Directory, for several months, maintained that it wanted no conquests beyond the natural frontiers except in order to obtain recognition of those frontiers in exchange. These very conquests increased the danger. The Directory made it a principle that its armies should live at the expense of the occupied countries, and should even send it part of their loot; it had already been observed in Belgium and the Rhineland that the population did not appreciate such costly liberty and that France could entrust the government of those regions only to revolutionaries; when peace was concluded, would they be handed back again to their enemies? Then again, the example of Dumouriez gave grounds for fearing that there might be generals who would carry out a personal policy in the occupied countries and proceed to make new conquests with the support of greedy contractors. The Committee of Public Safety had provided against this danger by subordinating the generals to the representatives on mission. The Directory replaced the latter with commissioners to the armies: Joubert and Alexandre for the armies of the North and of the Sambre and Meuse, Haussmann for the Army of the Rhine and Moselle, and Saliceti and Garrau for the Army of Italy. But in theory it granted them only a right of supervision. True, it was not long before it also entrusted them with a task of collecting war taxes, authorizing the conclusion of armistices, and putting down looting. It was inevitable that they should enter into conflict with the generals, the sole masters of the armies. Behind the representatives, there had been the revolutionary court; behind the commissioners, there was only the tottering authority of the Directory: they were sacrificed, and the generals did as they pleased. However, it was an unforseeable chance which determined the course of events. According to Carnot's plan, it was the armies of the Sambre and Meuse and of the Rhine and Moselle, under Jourdan and Moreau, which were to deal the decisive blow by marching on Vienna; those of the Alps and of Italy, under Kellerman and Schérer, being much weaker, were to conquer, if they could, northern Italy as a form of surety. But on 12 Ventôse, Bonaparte was substituted for Schérer.

He was born at Ajaccio in 1769, just after Corsica had been occupied by the French. His father, who accepted

French rule at an early date, obtained recognition for his nobility, and Napoleon was accordingly able to enter the Brienne Academy, and then the Military Academy, which he left as a second lieutenant in the Artillery. Poor and without any prospects, he owed everything to the Revolution, but, hating the French, he saw nothing in it at first but an opportunity to liberate Corsica and to play an important part there under Paoli. But the latter preferred the Posso di Borgo clan to the suspect Bonapartes, and when he broke with the Revolution and called in the English, the Bonapartes were expelled. It was then that Napoleon really naturalized himself in the service of the Montagnard Convention; he distinguished himself at the siege of Toulon and in the Army of Italy, in which he inspired the brilliant operations of Saorgio and Dego. Arrested for a while as a Robespierrist, and reduced to inactivity, he was put back into the saddle, on the thirteenth of Vendémiaire, as a result of the decisive support that he gave to Barras. Before leaving for Italy, he married Joséphine de Beauharnais, who had been the latter's mistress. It is hard to believe that he was ignorant of this, and that the influence she had retained did not help him; but he was passionately in love with her and there can be no doubt that Carnot appointed him deliberately.

Bonaparte had read Guibert, the prophet of the new war whose theories the Revolution had made applicable without Carnot or any general fully realizing the consequences. His genius was to derive a doctrine of war from them and to practice it with a mastery which has known no equal. In the Army of Italy, he had also studied—and what is more, on the spot—Maillebois' campaigns and Bourcet's book on mountain warfare. In his notes to the Committee of Public Safety in Year II and Year III, and in the instructions for Schérer which he inspired, the essential features of the Italian Campaign were already clearly delineated: it was necessary to aim at Austria, to put Piedmont out of action first of all in order to conquer Lombardy in safety, then, ignoring the peninsula, to march on Vienna across the Alps.

The Army of Italy occupied a large part of the Genoa Riviera and, since Schérer's victory at Loano, held the upper valley of the Tanaro, as well as the passes toward the two Bormidas. Bonaparte assembled 38,000 men to fall upon Colli's Piedmontese, whose active strength could not exceed 12,000 men; Beaulieu's 35,000 Austrians, still scattered in their winter quarters, seemed unlikely to be able to help him. In fact, when Saliceti sent a brigade toward Genoa, whose government he wished to intimidate in order to extract money from it, Beaulieu hurried up to stop him, but this step prevented him from concentrating his troops and helping Colli or his own subordinate Argenteau, whom he had ordered to cut off the French troops' retreat. Bonaparte began by getting rid of the latter, who was routed at Montenotte on April 12, driven out of Dago, and thrown back on Acqui. At the same time, Augereau was driving the Piedmontese out of Millesimo, while Serurier was descending the Tanaro; attacked on the sixteenth at Ceva and on the eighteenth at San Michele, Colli inflicted some bloody reverses on his opponent; but, with his flank constantly being turned, he had to retreat every time, and after finally being hustled out of Mondovi on the 21st, he fell back to cover Turin. The Piedmontese revolutionaries started agitating. The Court took fright, and on the twenty-eighth, an armistice was signed at Cherasco. Beaulieu had withdrawn to the north of the Po, behind the Ticino. Bonaparte took him in the rear by forcing the passage of the Po at Piacenza, but Beaulieu, suspecting the danger, was already in retreat. He escaped, leaving only a rear guard on the Adda: at Lodi, on May 10, the bridge was taken by force. Retracing his steps, Bonaparte entered Milan. After the King of Sardinia had signed a peace treaty on May 15, ceding Savoy and Nice, he set off again and without meeting any opposition reached the Mincio, which he crossed at Borghetto on May 30. The siege of Mantua began. Since Beaulieu had failed to respect the neutrality of Venetian territory, a convention handed Verona over to the French, and granted them right of way. The Dukes of Parma and Modena obtained armistices; Bologna and Ferrara were occupied without a shot being fired.

In Milan, Bonaparte's policy had already taken shape. He had allowed the formation of a club, promised independence and given the National Guard the tricolor cockade of Italy. But he had also demanded an indemnity of twenty million francs, payable by the rich; Saliceti took possession of the public coffers and the pawnshops which, in that region, served as safe deposits; the army lived off the country. The contradiction became immediately apparent: the revolt broke out and was harshly suppressed, especially at Pavia. France could therefore count only on the Italian Jacobins, whose declared object was to revolutionize the whole of Italy in order to make it a unified republic. The Directory announced entirely contrary intentions: the Italian conquest was simply a pawn which had to be thoroughly exploited before it was handed back. It was so preoccupied with the question of booty that it ordered Bonaparte to leave Kellermann standing guard over Lombardy, and to go and hold the peninsula for ransom. At a moment when the Austrians were going to return to the attack, this order was ridiculous, and it had the further drawback of allowing Bonaparte to test his strength without any risk to himself: he offered his resignation and the Directory promptly capitulated. Admittedly, its wishes were partly satisfied. The Pope and the Dukes of Parma and Modena were forced to pay heavy indemnities, as well as to hand over manuscripts and objects of art chosen by a special commission. A division occupied Leghorn, the main center of British trade.

Bonaparte seems to have extracted about fifty million francs from Italy, and the Directory received about ten million. But the general's emancipation was only accelerated as a result. After conquering Italy, his dominating genuis brooked no impediments in that country. His army became his chattel; it lived as it pleased in a land of milk and honey, and he had granted it half its pay in metallic currency, which the Directory could not obtain for the others. He had gathered around him a horde of contractors and individuals with an eye to profit—like Haller, who became the Paymaster to the Army, or like that Hamelin, whom Josephine had brought along in return for an allowance, and whose memoirs are so enlightening. What did he intend to do with Lombardy: Make it a fief where he would settle down after the war? Whoever thought that did not understand his nature. He was the man of the moment endowed with an unequaled realism, but an object attained was never anything but the means of aiming at another which his ardent imagination had already conceived. On the evening of the Battle of Lodi, he had become aware of himself: "I saw the world sinking beneath me as if I had been swept up into the air."

The Directory did not worry, for it was a good summer for the Republic. Instead of concentrating the forces intended for the invasion of Germany, Carnot had ordered Jourdan and Moreau to operate separately; however, the drawbacks of this procedure did not appear right away. Jourdan having taken the offensive on May 31, to the right of the Rhine, the Archduke Charles repulsed him without evacuating the left bank; but at the news of Bonaparte's victories, Wurmser, who was facing Moreau, was sent to Italy with some of his troops. Charles, left in sole command, abandoned the Palatinate, and when Moreau had finally crossed the Rhine, on June 24. Jourdan returned to the attack. While Wartensleben fell back before him as far as the Naab, Moreau drove the Archduke back toward Bavaria, and ended up by reaching Munich. In Italy, Wurmser enjoyed no success. His troops, coming down from the Tyrol on both sides of Lake Garda, were beaten at Lonato and, on August 5, at Castiglione. Returning to Trent, he hit on the idea of trying to reach Mantua by the valley of the Brenta; but Bonaparte was already in pursuit, and on September 15 he was forced to take refuge in the fortress. The Directory had just concluded an alliance with Spain, thus depriving the English fleet of the bases which had enabled it to dominate the Mediterranean. It left that sea after evacuating Corsica, which the French reoccupied in October; Bonaparte was thus safe from British intervention. Moreover, since July the French had been planning a landing in Ireland in co-operation with Wolf Tone, who was preparing an insurrection there. This succession of blows persuaded Pitt to offer to negotiate, and the Directory agreed to hold a conference at Lille.

Meanwhile Bonaparte was going his own way. Saliceti

and Garrau, both good Jacobins, were helping him in this without worrying about their government. A Lombard legion had been created; the senate of Reggio asked for help against the Duke of Modena. Bonaparte repudiated the armistice and, in agreement with the commissioners, summoned a congress which, on October 15, grouped Modena and the Legations taken from the Pope in a Cispadane Republic. The general nonetheless wanted to rid himself of the commissioners. Already Italy was becoming exhausted and the army's condition was worsening again; Saliceti having been sent to Corsica, Garrau remained as the sole target for recrimination. On October 25, Bonaparte took a decisive step: he put Baraguey, who was in command in Lombardy, in control of the whole administration of the country, without any mention of the commissioner.

Meanwhile the Republic's affairs were now taking a turn for the worse. The Armies of Germany having made no attempt to link up, the Archduke left Latour facing Moreau, joined Wartensleben, and marched on Nürnberg. Jourdan, taken in the rear, retreated; the slowness of his adversary enabled him to regain the Lahn with only slight losses, but there he was attacked and routed, and he recrossed the Rhine at the end of September. Moreau had only belatedly realized the danger he was running. Returning to the Black Forest, he learned that Charles was hurrying up to cut off his retreat and had to turn off along Hell Valley; his adversary was incapable of either concentrating his forces or of making haste, and he was able to cross the Rhine at Hüningen on October 26. The Austrians were now free for the most part to go into Italy; instead they stubbornly persisted in trying to take the bridgeheads of Kehl and Hüningen, which the French defended throughout the winter. All the same, a new commander, Alvinczy, took the offensive against Bonaparte, reached the gates of Verona, and repulsed every attack at Caldiero; however, as a result of the furious fighting at Arcole between November 14 and 17, Bonaparte succeeded in forcing him to retreat, but he had narrowly escaped disaster and the moral and material condition of his troops was pitiful. Soon afterwards, on December 19, Malmesbury, Pitt's envoy, not receiving the full powers with which the Directory had insisted that he should be furnished in advance, was asked to leave France. The Irish expedition, which had been placed under Hoche's command, had just set sail: it was scattered by a storm and returned to port in discomfiture. Then, on February 14, 1797, Jervis defeated the Spanish fleet off Cape St. Vincent and obtained access to the Mediterranean once more.

Bonaparte was thrown into relief as much by the setbacks of the other generals as by his own victories; he remained the Directory's only hope. After all, the defeated generals had not been much more docile than he. Kléber and Bernadotte had had the impudence, in full retreat, to tender their resignations to Jourdan and abandon him. Beurnonville, who took Jourdan's place, came into conflict with Commissioner Alexandre. Moreau had granted an armistice to Württemberg without consulting Haussmann, and returned to France on the worst possible terms with the latter. The Directory, thoroughly disheartened, dismissed the commissioners to the armies. Everywhere, the generals were left in sole command. Then again, the setbacks of the autumn had given a hold to Carnot and his friends to the Right. Already, he had secretly tried to get in touch with Thugut; in November, he insisted that Clarke, the head of his military office, be sent to Italy to negotiate an armistice. Ordered to investigate the state of the army and the conquered region as well, Clarke was rapidly won over by Bonaparte; moreover, the Directory, while confirming its intention to exchange Lombardy for the Rhineland, instructed Clarke to consult Bonaparte about the peace conditions.

Soon matters improved once more. Alvinczy had descended the Adige with 50,000 men, while Provera was advancing from Friuli towards Mantua. On January 14, 1797, on the Plateau of Rivoli, Bonaparte repulsed the Austrian columns which attacked him and drove them back into the mountains; the next day, Joubert scattered or captured what remained of them. On the sixteenth, Bonaparte, who had immediately set off again with the Masséna division, forced Provera to capitulate. Mantua finally surrendered. The excitement of victory combined with the reaction inspired by the Brottier conspiracy to divert the Directory from the path it had invariably followed until then: Clarke received orders to defend the Cispadane Republic, and on 15 Pluviôse Bonaparte was sent the famous letter, already mentioned, which urged him to destroy the temporal power of the Papacy. However, a rectification followed before long. Bonaparte and Clarke, having asked for permission to give a constitution to Lombardy, were merely authorized, on April 7, to create a provisional administration, emanating only from the general and not committing the Directory. Then the Army of the Sambre and Meuse, now under Hoche's command, crossed the Rhine again on April 16 and 18, and was soon in front of Frankfurt; on the twentieth, Moreau also crossed the river. An order was sent to Clarke to postpone any armistice; Germany was going to become the main theater of war again. It was too late: Bonaparte had already cut the Gordian knot.

After the fall of Mantua, he had marched on Rome, but without meaning to go very far: Clarke having shown him his orders, he knew that if he did not sign the peace himself, it would return Lombardy, and he regarded the surrender of Lombardy as an insult to himself. He therefore had to reach Vienna before the Armies of the Rhine. He lost no time in coming to terms with the Pope at Tolentino, demanding only a few million as well as Avignon and the Legations. On March 20, he took the offensive. Superior in numbers this time to the Austrians, who were now under the command of Archduke Charles, he reached the Tarvisio without much difficulty, from which point the Masséna division advanced as far as the foot of the Semmering: at Leoben, on April 7, Thugut's plenipotentiaries presented themselves to treat for peace. It was Bonaparte who, as early as March 30, had sent the Archduke an offer to negotiate. If he had been eager to forestall the armies of the Rhine, he was nonetheless worried by their inactivity, which could give the Austrians time to overwhelm him— all the more so in that his rear was no longer safe. It seems that, considering that it would be impossible to carry out his plan without offering Austria a bait, he had decided, even before taking the field, to offer her part of the Venetian States; in March, his subordinates provoked a revolution at Brescia and at Bergamo, and it is difficult to believe that they would have ventured to do this without his permission. Next, they tried to stir up the Terra Firma against the Most Serene Republic, but it was against the French that the peasants, irritated by the military occupation and indoctrinated by the clergy and nobility, took up arms. On

88

April 17, the garrison at Verona was taken by surprise and some of the troops were killed. Bonaparte was now in a very hazardous position. No less than the desire to appear at all costs as the peacemaker, and no less than the pride which attached him to his conquests, it explains the extraordinary choice which he offered Thugut: either Istria, Dalmatia, and the whole of the Terra Firma as far as the Oglio, though with the exception of Venice, if he ceded Belgium; or else just Venetia and then only as far as the Tagliamento, if he abandoned the Rhineland as well as Belgium. This was tantamount to dictating Thugut's reply. Without any authority, and without consulting Clarke whom he had been careful to send off to Turin, Bonaparte signed both the armistice and the preliminaries of the peace of Leoben on April 18. By this treaty the Republic went beyond its natural frontier of the Alps and, following the scandalous example of the Polish partitions, sacrificed an independent state to its own convenience, handing Italians over to Germans; and all this without reaching the Rhine, the "natural frontier" that it considered the most important of all.

Bonaparte had immediately sent off couriers to halt the armies of the Rhine, and had taken care to see that the news of the treaty spread before the Directory itself knew the terms. Immediately after the Royalist elections, could the Directory defy both public opinion and the general? It did not dare to do so, and ratified an agreement which dishonored the Revolution. Installed at Mombello, in the palace of the Crivellis, Bonaparte now appeared to the whole world as a true sovereign. He raised Lombardy to the dignity of a "Cisalpine Republic," gave her a constitution, joined Valtellina to her and tried to persuade Valais to grant her

a road to France by way of the Simplon Pass, but in vain
—a failure which promptly gave him the idea of interven-
ing in Switzerland. He had also thought of extending the
Cisalpine Republic as far as the sea by dismembering the
Republic of Genoa, but the Genoese patriots forestalled
him by carrying out their own revolution which they placed
under his protection.

His imagination turned toward the east: out of the spoils
of Venice, he had retained the Ionian Isles in order to get
in touch with the Ottoman Empire, and he suggested to
the Directory that he should seize Malta. However, the
final treaty with Austria still had to be concluded, and he
had explained that he hoped to take advantage of it to keep
Mantua and to obtain the Rhine. He had declared war on
Venice of his own accord on May 2; on the twelfth, the
democrats in Venice had overthrown the oligarchy and let
in the French; on the sixteenth, Bonaparte had negotiated
with the representatives of the government which had
ceased to exist, a device which had enabled him to avoid
recognizing the new government. Now in a position to
hand over Venice herself, he reopened negotiations with
Thugut. The latter raised no objections to ceding the Rhineland, counting on obtaining not only Venice, but also the
Legations. Discussions opened at Udine.

Abandoned by Austria, horrified by the mutiny of her
sailors, and at grips with the Irish, England, for her part,
had sent Malmesbury back to Lille, where negotiations had
been resumed on July 7. The Directory made some large
claims, but its chief demand was neither more nor less than
that the English restore to France and her allies the colonies
they had seized. This did not appeal to Pitt, who wanted to
keep at least Ceylon and Trinidad. The Directory, however,

had not said its last word, for it exerted strong pressure on
Holland to persuade her to cede Ceylon. But at Lille as at
Udine, the negotiations came to nothing. This was because
Thugut and Pitt knew what was happening in Paris.

The generals of the Republic had never ceased to be
abused by the newspapers of the Right. Now they were
subjected to attacks in the Councils too. Disposing of the resources of the conquered countries as they pleased, without
furnishing accounts to anyone, they lent themselves to
criticism; Hoche was accused of having set up a Black
Fund in order to prepare for a *coup d'état*. But it was the
Venetian affair which set the cat among the pigeons. The
"Veronese Easter" had reduced the Right to silence for a
moment; but shortly afterwards the *Quotidienne* published
some letters from Mallet du Pan, a publicist in the pay of
England and Austria, stigmatizing its shameful inertia. On
5 Messidor (June 23), Dumolard, in a passionate speech,
made out a well-founded indictment of Bonaparte. Of foreign inspiration, it nonetheless allowed the Directory to
consider the Anglo-Royalist plot as being also an Austrian
plot. Pastoret, for his part, bitterly criticized the measures
taken against those neutral countries which placed themselves at the service of English trade, on the ground that
France was thus running the risk of war with the United
States. Dandré went further: he promised Wickham to
help British policy, admittedly reserving the right to protect
French interests, though it is not clear how he interpreted
those interests. Thugut tried to take advantage of feeling on
the Right and sent to Paris an envoy who, in August, met
Carnot and Barthélemy; they declared that they were powerless to help, since the triumvirs no longer consulted them.
At Lille, Maret, one of the Directory's representatives, ad-

vised Malmesbury to play for time, since the victory of the
Councils was imminent; he was hand-in-glove with Talleyrand and, thanks to him, was able to reveal to the English
the conditions of the treaty just signed with Portugal. Some
suspicious individuals, who claimed to represent Barras and
Talleyrand, offered their services for money. Pitt too decided to wait.

After the elections of Year V, a close connection had
thus been established between the foreign policy of the
Republic and its internal situation. If the Directory suc-
cumbed, the Republic's foreign enemies would triumph at
small cost to themselves. But the Right, by attacking the
generals, had dictated their attitude. After reading Dumolard's speech, Bonaparte exploded in fury. In reality, he
played a double game as usual: he went on corresponding
with Carnot, and, on the advice of his aide-de-camp La-
valette, who had come to Paris, he did not send the Directory the three million francs he had promised. But Hoche
was incapable of such devices, and, since he was within
reach, it is he who would have carried out the *coup d'état*
if the Directory had been more cunning. Would the fate of
the Republic have been different as a result? It is pleasant
to think so, although the pestilential influence of the war
of conquest may not have spared even Hoche. With Marceau
and Kléber, he has remained dear to Republican tradition
on account of his gay and generous impetuosity, his youth-
ful lower-class enthusiasm for the Revolution. Around the
memory of the soldier-citizen, whom death carried off a few
days after the eighteenth of Fructidor, there float those
Beethovian strains which express a regret for a noble hope
left unfulfilled. It is to him that the *Eroica* should have
been dedicated.

The soldiers followed their generals. Many of them retained a fierce loyalty to the Revolution and to the Republic which now incarnated it. Having shed their blood for these ideals, they considered themselves entitled to protect them against the civilians who elected Royalists: Revolution and Republic were their property. Yet there must be no illusions on this score: the armies also followed the example of their leaders, and the proof of that can be seen in the fact that the Army of the Rhine and Moselle imitated to only a limited degree those of Italy and of the Sambre and Meuse. Moreau had kept secret the correspondence of Condé's envoys, which had been captured in an Austrian wagon and which revealed the treason of his friend Pichegru; during the campaign, he had treated respectfully émigrés caught bearing arms; and he shut his eyes to Royalist propaganda. The transformation of the armies explains the growing ascendancy of their generals. Since Year II, the soldier had been increasingly reduced to passive obedience; he no longer took part in the election of his officers; the jury no longer played any part in military law; since the law of 13 Brumaire, Year V (November 3, 1796), there had no longer been a soldier among the judges; and the merging of volunteers and conscripts had subordinated both to the discipline of the line. Then again, it can be argued that the soldiers of the Directory, distinguished by the desertion of their fellows, were in a sense volunteers. They had remained because they loved war and its adventures, or because they would not have known what to do outside the regiment; little by little, they became separate from the rest of the nation, all the more so in that, since the *levée en masse*, there had been no more conscription. Professional soldiers, and encamped on foreign soil into the bargain—how could they have failed to turn to their commanders?

But they never became a Pretorian Guard. The Republic never knew a *pronunciamiento*: soldiers and generals only carried out a *coup d'état*, on the eighteenth of Brumaire as on the eighteenth of Fructidor, in response to an appeal by the bourgeoisie.

CHAPTER SEVEN

The Eighteenth of Fructidor

The Right was getting ready to suppress the political societies when, on 28 Messidor (July 16, 1797), it learned of the dismissal of the ministers it trusted; like the dismissal of Necker in 1789, the event seemed to herald a *coup d'état*. Anxiety grew when, the following day, Petiet revealed that troops were approaching the capital; two days later, the deputies known as inspectors of the hall, whose duty it was to police the constitutional precinct of the Councils, confirmed that some cavalry regiments were reported to be at La Ferte-Alais, near Corbeil, a place which appeared to be within the constitutional belt. Pichegru and his friends had gone to ask for explanations, and countless groups discussed what measures should be taken. The indictment of the triumvirs seemed the only effective step. But what if they resisted? It had to be admitted that force was on their side. Nonetheless, it seems that Pichegru and Vaublanc came to an agreement with Carnot, who was then president of the Directory. Called to the bar, he was to throw the blame on the triumvirs, and an indictment would have followed; perhaps Rochecot, who was then in Paris with a band of Chouans, vainly proposing to take the Directory by force, would have intervened. But when, on 2 Thermidor (July 20), the message arrived which, without explaining why the troops had been sent, attributed their presence so close to Paris to a mistake, it was noted that Carnot had signed it. This was because Barras had shown him the document sent by Bonaparte which furnished proof of Pichegru's treason. Carnot, utterly taken aback, had changed his attitude; shortly afterwards, on the anniversary of the tenth of August, he made it clear in his speech that he would not lend himself to a Restoration. This *coup de théâtre* threw the Right into confusion.

The triumvirs, for their part, were not ready. Arriving in Paris, Hoche had been taken to task by Carnot; having imagined that the Directors were in agreement, he did not know what to reply and flew into a temper against Barras who had earned him this humiliation. Then Willot pointed out that, since he was under forty, the general could not be a minister, and a substitute had to be found. The Directory allowed the clubs to be suppressed without making any comment and Barras sent Fabre de l'Aude to propose an agreement to Pichegru. The offer was rejected, but on 8 Thermidor (July 26), Pichegru, in the conclusion of his report, confined himself to laying down the limits of the constitutional belt, in order to avoid any future error, and to banning any movement of troops from one military subdivision to another without a decree from the Directory.

This was only an interlude. It was not long before news came of the threatening proclamation which Bonaparte had read out to his soldiers on July 14, and the still more violent addresses from different divisions of his army; the Army of the Sambre and Meuse lost no time in sending similar addresses. On 3 Thermidor (July 21), the Directory had legalized the movement of the troops in a decree ordering reinforcements to be sent to Brest: they set off again under Hoche, who had left Paris after a reconciliation with Barras. His friend Chérin was put in command of the Directory guard, and it was he who prepared the *coup d'état*; Augereau, sent to Paris by Bonaparte and appointed commander of the seventeenth military division, undertook to carry it out. Under various pretexts, detachments, arms and munitions came into Paris. Money was scarce: Hoche provided a little and so, probably, did the contractors whom the Councils' attacks had ranged behind the government. Retired officers arrived from all sides and the hunting of "black collars," in other words fops, started again in Paris.

The Right, on the recommendation of Willot and Delarue, replied only with fresh demands for explanations about the approach of the troops and the seditious addresses of the armies. At this the Directory openly took the offensive, with its message of 23 Thermidor (August 10). Explaining, this time, the march of the troops by the preparations at Brest and thus assuming responsibility for it, it reduced the incident, as it had done from the beginning, to an insignificant mistake in the mapping out of a route.

As for the addresses, though they were doubtless illegal, the indignation which had dictated them was legitimate. Who were the real culprits? The counterrevolutionaries who murdered Republicans and those who, in the Councils, did their best to support them, while reducing the government to impotence by leaving the Treasury empty. Then the presidency fell to La Revellière, and on 10 Fructidor (August 27), receiving the envoys of the Cisalpine Republic, he made a speech that was even more provocative: "The Directory will not treat with the enemies of the Republic."

The majority, growing increasingly anxious, went on discussing without coming to any decision. On 25 Thermidor (August 12), it had admittedly authorized the reconstitution of the crack companies of the National Guard, the riflemen and the grenadiers: this was in order to rearm the bourgeoisie of the big towns so as to repeat the *journée* of Vendémiaire. Pichegru declared that the arsenals would provide the necessary arms and equipment, but in spite of Carnot, the triumvirs did not give effect to this law. The Five Hundred passed a resolution to reinstate in the gendarmerie the officers who had been excluded as suspects since 1791. The Ancients rejected it.

Two other resolutions would undoubtedly have been effective: the Guard of the Legislature was to be placed under the discretionary authority of the inspectors of the hall and removed from that of Augereau and the Directory; and retired officers would only be able to draw their pension in their place of residence, a measure which would oblige them to leave Paris. But the Ancients postponed a decision and the Five Hundred showed no greater diligence in respect of two other points: guarantees to be given to officers against the right of dismissal, which was invested in the Directory, and the attribution to the criminal court of the Seine of all trials for offenses against the security of the State.

The inspectors of the hall, usurping powers which transformed them into a sort of executive committee of the majority, could have organized means of action; Rovère formed a police force and Willot recruited volunteers. For his part, Dandré distributed arms, kept the Philanthropic Institute on the alert, and asked Wickham for money. Pichegru ended up by agreeing to have recourse to the Chouans. As anxiety grew, it was decided on 17 Fructidor (September 3) that Vaublanc should demand an indictment. This would inevitably have been the signal for action. But the Directory acted first.

In the night of 17-18 Fructidor, the triumvirs, after summoning the ministers Augereau and Chérin, made final arrangements; at dawn, the alarm gun was fired and the city was placed under military occupation. Posters denounced the Anglo-Royalist plot and backed up the denunciation with Duverne de Presle's revelations and Antraigue's document. A decree announced that anyone who tried to instigate the restoration of the Monarchy or of the Constitution of 1793 would be shot without any form of trial. A group of deputies, led by Pastoret, presented itself at the Tuileries and was dispersed. Nobody tried to take up arms. Right at the start, Pichegru, Willot and Ramel had been arrested at the Tuileries by Augereau. A few others, including Barthélemy, who refused to take flight as the triumvirs had hoped he would, were taken with them to the Temple. Carnot, whom they hated, had managed to make his escape.

The Councils had been transferred to the Medical

School and to the Odéon, where nothing was ready for them. By the time a quorum had been formed, it was late in the day. Most of the deputies were in a state of consternation, even the Left being unable to avoid the realization that the Constitution had been struck a mortal blow. But it was too late to hesitate. During the night the Five Hundred passed the exceptional law proposed by the triumvirs, and the Ancients ratified it on 19 Fructidor, Year V (September 5, 1797). On the twenty-second, they passed a second law against the press. A few other laws followed later.

Altogether, forty-nine departments had their elections totally annulled, and others their representation cut down. The south of France, except for Provence, was the least affected. During the following months, the Directory also dismissed a great many administrations. Sixty-five individuals were sentenced to transportation to Guiana, including Carnot, Barthélemy, Ramel, forty-two members of the Five Hundred, eleven members of the Ancients, and three of the accused in the Brottier conspiracy. Fifteen of them, joined voluntarily by Barthélemy's valet, were taken away on the twentieth in iron cages. Two others went the same way a little later. Eight died in Guiana, including Gibert-Desmolières, Tronson-Ducoudray, Aubry, and Rovère. A few escaped, notably Pichegru. The others did not return until after the eighteenth of Brumaire. Altogether, 177 deputies were eliminated and their places left vacant. Of those who had been spared, some retired from public life: Dupont de Nemours resigned; Doulcet went on leave; the others, Thibaudeau for example, withdrew into silence. The opposition did not disappear, but it was decapitated and reduced to a minority.

The émigrés, even those who had been provisionally struck off, were given a fortnight to leave France under pain of death. The law of 3 Brumaire, Year IV was revived, and indeed aggravated; the relatives of émigrés were deprived of the right to vote. The repeal of the laws of 1792 and 1793 against the clergy was annulled, and the deportees who had returned to France were ordered to go back into exile; but the death penalty which those laws imposed upon them and which, as the Directory had pointed out several times, had led the courts to prefer acquittal to conviction, was replaced by deportation to Guiana. In return, the Directory was given the right to sentence any priest to deportation by an individual decree; moreover, in confirmation of the law of 7 Vendémiaire, Year IV, the promise of submission to the laws was replaced by the oath of hatred for the Monarchy and the Constitution of 1793.

The clubs were authorized once more, but the press was hard hit. Forty-two papers had been suppressed and their proprietors, editors and staff condemned to deportation, a fate which, it is true, nearly all escaped. The press was placed for a year at the disposal of the police, as was permitted by the Constitution.

The authority of the Directory increased considerably. In the majority of departments, as a result of dismissals and the annulment of the elections, there were vacancies in the courts and the administrative bodies: the Directory was given authority to fill these vacancies, in the administrations until the elections of Year VI, and in the courts until the normal end of the mandate. The Court of Appeal was likewise purged; only the Treasury escaped, probably because Ramel had been compromised with it in the Dijon Company affair. Finally, the Directory resumed the power to proclaim martial law when and where it thought fit.

The eighteenth of Fructidor consecrated the failure of the constitutional and liberal experiment attempted by the Thermidorians: the Republic had returned to a dictatorship, and since it was the Directory which had taken the initiative, it was the Directory which benefited as a result. The authority of the Legislature, already very limited, would be reduced still further, a state of affairs to which the deputies resigned themselves no more than the Convention had done after the thirty-first of May. Of further-reaching but no less decisive consequence was the influence implicitly attributed from now on to the army and its generals: the soldier had saved the Republic, and he regarded it more than ever as his property. Moreover, he was immediately assured that his importance could only grow in the future, because the eighteenth of Fructidor also set the Republic on the road to a new war.

It was inevitable that the foreign policy of France should be affected by the *coup d'état*, since the Royalists' collusion with the enemy was one of its contributory factors. Reubell immediately resumed supreme control of foreign affairs; the diplomatic staff was changed and Talleyrand took refuge in submission. At Lille, new plenipotentiaries called upon Malmesbury to restore unreservedly all the colonies of France and her allies, and negotiations were broken off as a result. In the Rhineland, Hoche being dead, the plan that he had supported for a Cisrhenan Republic was abandoned. As Thugut, now resigned to treating for peace, had sent Cobenzl to negotiate with Bonaparte, who was installed near Udine, in the Castle of Passariano, the Directory indicated that it wanted the Rhine frontier, and, since the Republic of Venice was to be restored, granted Austria only Istria and Dalmatia. Preparations for a winter campaign were set on foot. Bonaparte admittedly expected to improve the conditions provided for at Leoben, but he was well aware that a winter campaign could be waged only in Germany, and he had no intention of being thrust into the background by a *coup d'état* which he had helped to bring about. Setting himself up as arbiter, he offered Thugut, of his own accord, the Venetian territory as far as the Adige, except for the Ionian Isles; in return, he demanded Austria's support for the cession of the left bank of the Rhine, which was to be negotiated at Rastatt with the Empire, but was to exclude the region of Cologne. Cobenzl ended up by agreeing, and the treaty was signed on October 18, 1797, at Passariano, although it bears the name of the little village of Campo-Formio where the ceremony had originally been planned to take place. The Directory was utterly dismayed; but, apart from the fact that after the *coup d'état* it had countless difficulties to overcome, how could it break with the imperious general, who now had no rivals? Hoche was dead; and Moreau, who at the very moment of the eighteenth of Fructidor had decided to hand over the papers which compromised Pichegru, had been put aside as being more than unreliable. The treaty was ratified.

The Venetian iniquity was thus confirmed and even amplified, since Venice too had been handed over to Austria. Moreover, from the diplomatic point of view, the Rhineland provisions were disastrous. Thugut had retained the region of Cologne for the Empire, because it was there that Prussia's possessions were situated, with the result that that country would not be entitled to any indemnity; it could therefore be expected that in the Diet she would oppose the cession and would also draw away from France. A fresh offensive was thus likely on the part of Austria, whose Italian ambitions had been partially disappointed.

Nothing was more calculated to suggest fresh encroachments beyond the natural frontiers, which indeed had not yet been reached in the region of the Rhine. If the war was to be resumed—and in point of fact it was still going on with England—it was important that France should be sure of the countries which she had taken under her protection and which served her as a glacis; the Batavian Republic and the Cisalpine Republic were not slow to become aware of this. In order to link the latter to France, Bonaparte thought of taking over Valais, though it was even simpler to invade Piedmont. Everywhere the Directory's new ambassadors—Delacroix at The Hague, Ginguené at Turin, and even Truguet at Madrid—started speaking like masters.

Nor was that all. Although officially no appeal had been made to the Jacobins, the *coup d'état* of the eighteenth of Fructidor had been carried out with their help; and, by insistently denouncing the Royalist peril, the Directory had reawakened the revolutionary spirit and at the same time aroused the enthusiasm for universal propaganda and war to the death against the tyrants which was virtually inseparable from it. It was in Year VI that the Republicans began priding themselves on belonging to the "Great Nation" whose mission was to free the world. La Revellière was susceptible to this idealism; Barras' greedy, restless spirit was not averse to upheavals; Reubell joined with them in welcoming the prospect of the fall of the Papacy, and, linked as an Alsatian with the democrats of Basle, he was predisposed in favor of intervention in Switzerland. Finally, it went without saying that generals and contractors, out of natural inclination and personal interest, would everywhere give their support to the propaganda which made them indispensable.

Less than six months after the eighteenth of Fructidor, the French were in Rome and at Berne with the approval or at the instigation of Bonaparte, who shortly afterwards would finally provoke, by setting off for Egypt, the formation of the Second Coalition.

CHAPTER EIGHT

The Directorial Terror

If the government of the second Directory, as the historians call it, was regarded as a dictatorship, that is not only because it was a "revolutionary" government, established in violation of the Constitution, but also, and rather, because the eighteenth of Fructidor inaugurated a new Terror. It remains to be seen whether the Directorial Terror revived the "coercive force" with the same severity which made the Committee of Public Safety omnipotent.

The revolutionary court was not re-established, and Bailleul proposed in vain the creation of a special court for the crime of conspiracy. However, there could be no question of using the High Court, which was slow and unreliable; the Directory had recourse when necessary to the criminal courts. It was the criminal court of the Seine which sentenced the Royalist singer Ange Pitou to deportation, and that of the Rhône which sent Allier and Surville to the scaffold, but this jurisdiction was not reliable either. Every dictatorship, and the Terror which is its indispensable complement, presuppose an exceptional jurisdiction. Against the Grenelle rebels, the Directory had already had recourse to military justice; widespread use had been made of it in Year II and it remained competent to deal with émigrés and deportees. The disturbances which followed the eighteenth of Fructidor made it possible to extend its use to a considerable degree. These disturbances were serious only in a few places—at Pont-Saint-Esprit, where the Baron de Saint-Christol was in complete control for two days, at Carpentras, at Montauban—but these rebellions provided an opportunity to set up a large number of military commissions. Then again, the Directorial dictatorship, like all dictatorships, was a police regime. Passports were reintroduced. The Legislature did not authorize domiciliary visits until Messidor, Year IV, and then for only a month, but the Directory went ahead without its permission; roundups were also carried out in the country districts. Under the Constitution, the Directory could order arrests through administrative channels under the pretext of conspiracy, but its commissioners did not possess this right, any more than did the departmental or municipal administrators; yet this is what they did, with or without the authority of the Minister of Police. They even drew up lists of suspects to be imprisoned should the occasion arise; these prisoners were released after varying times without even having been interrogated. Postal secrecy was not respected any more than individual liberty. As for the freedom of the press, it was officially suspended; the censorship was not re-established any more than it had been in Year II, but the Minister of Police had a census of papers carried out, and on the basis of his reports, the Directory suppressed a considerable number of them—sixteen at once, for example, on 27 Frimaire, Year VI (December 17, 1797). Admittedly they soon started reappearing under other names, but, reduced to extreme prudence, they had become insipid; moreover, many of their contributors were affected by the deportation order decreed on 22 Fructidor. Books were likewise seized. As for the theaters, Audouin, in April, 1798, got the Five Hundred to confer on the Directory the right to control them. Lamarque had protested against this increase of power for the Executive; nonetheless, he had asked for a law to fix the number of theaters and impose a host of restrictions on them. The Ancients rejected the resolution, but the Five Hundred did not take up Lamarque's plan, so that the police retained their arbitrary powers; in January, 1799, the Central Administration of the Seine gave orders for the existing repertory to be submitted to it and for all new plays to be presented to it in future.

Finally, administrative pressure increased as a result of the fact that dismissals and the annulment of elections reinforced centralization. In the Sarthe, for example, out of 807 agents and assistants, 584 had had their election quashed. Some of them were irregularly reinstated by the remaining minority; but the Directory dismissed another 290, so that in the end 599, or three-quarters of the total, were replaced, generally speaking to the satisfaction of the central power.

Two categories of individuals were the special targets of the Directorial Terror: the émigrés, as well as their relatives, and the priests. The case of the émigrés was clear, but, in the Councils themselves, attention was drawn several times to the danger of excessive repression. There were a good many errors in the list; the Directory had full power to add to it and was extremely slow to strike names off. Meanwhile it opposed any attenuation of the law of 19 Fructidor, maintaining that in cases of dispute the courts should suspend sentence until an administrative decision was reached: it is true that the military commissions acted with circumspection and that more than once the local administrations intervened in favor of the accused. However, the commissions had at least 160 people shot, including a few women, principally in the southeast, and in most cases during Year VI. To these must be added the death sentences passed by the criminal courts, which have not been counted. But emigration was not always the only ground for indictment: Rochecot, Trion, Allier, and Surville were also conspirators and rebels. As for the law of 3 Brumaire, Year IV, it henceforth caused less controversy. It was enforced against only one deputy, after which it was not mentioned again in the Councils; but this was because the persons concerned, taking the hint, henceforth took refuge in abstention. The relatives of émigrés continued to be unable to dispose of their property unless they agreed to a division of the anticipated succession, the Ancients having rejected the resolution which, before the eighteenth of Fructidor, had repealed the law of 12 Floréal, Year III.

The situation of the clergy was not as clear as that of the émigrés. In December, Chollet told the Five Hundred that there was still uncertainty about the laws of 1792 and 1793, since some people considered that they were still in force; he protested at the possible enforcement of the death penalty against deportees who had returned to France, and went much further in proposing that nothing more should be required of the clergy, even the non-juring priests, than the oath of hatred for the Monarchy. He did not win his case; Delbrel, however, obtained a decision that a commission would examine the modifications called for by considerations of humanity. There was no further mention of the subject; when, in Year VII, Briot demanded that all deportees should be considered as émigrés, his proposal was rejected. This suggests that the Five Hundred implicitly confirmed the substitution of deportation to Guiana for the death penalty in the case of deportees who had returned to France. Moreover, in Year VII, Duval, the Minister of Police, indicated in a circular that deportees who had returned home were liable only to deportation to Guiana. Unfortunately for them, many administrations had entered them on the list of émigrés, and as a result 41 were executed. Many others might have suffered the same fate, but the military commissions acquitted them or at least hesitated, in which case the administrations, on being consulted, frequently declared that the deportee, having left France in obedience to the law, could not be considered an émigré. The aforementioned circular by Duval confirmed that this was the case if the accused was listed with the endorsement "deportee," and that if this endorsement was missing he was entitled to dispute the inscription. Moreover, the example of Finistère reveals that the law of 19 Fructidor was enforced in an arbitrary fashion: some deportees who had returned to France, and who had complied with the law by asking for their passports, were promptly sent off to Rochefort, and some of them were put on ships for Guiana; another man was shipped off as liable to deportation without any sentence or administrative decree stating this to be the case.

Again, the priests who had taken the required oaths could be sentenced to deportation to Guiana by a Directorial decree; they were particularly exposed to this danger if they now refused the oath of hatred for the Monarchy. The government's obligation to issue a special decree for each individual was an illusory safeguard, and, in the case of the Belgian priests, no attention was paid to it: 9,234 of them were sentenced *en masse*.

In the rest of the Republic, between seventeen and eighteen hundred priests seem to have been sentenced, either as deportees who had returned to France or by Directorial decree. But very few of them set sail for Guiana. One of the ships was captured by the English; two others went off with 263 priests, of whom 156 died in Guiana. Of the others, 920 remained on the Isle of Ré and 192 on the Isle of Oléron, including 348 Belgians and one Rhinelander. Out of nearly eleven thousand priests liable to deportation, therefore, only a little over a tenth were arrested and only twenty-five in every thousand were eventually transported. Moreover, those who were infirm or over sixty years of age were interned in special houses. The life of the interned priests on the islands and on the mainland was very hard, and death claimed a considerable number of them, a fact which can be partly explained by their age.

Instituted on the eighteenth of Fructidor, the Directorial Terror was aimed at the Royalists, and it cannot be denied that it was quite effective: until Year VII, they were unable to attempt any serious insurrection. "Surveillance reached such a pitch," wrote Tercier, the Chouan of the Sarthe, "that there was no longer any safety anywhere." Allier and Surville, who had taken command of the Royalists in the Ardèche, were speedily defeated and executed. However, armed bands continued to roam the countryside without being easily distinguishable from brigands proper. Consequently, on 13 Nivôse, Year VI (January 18, 1798), a new exceptional law referred acts of brigandage liable to the death penalty to the military commissions, if they had been committed by two or more persons, though it left the preliminary examination to the ordinary magistrates. This was a considerable step toward provostal justice and clearly pointed the way toward the extraordinary courts of the Consulate.

If it had been left to certain members of the Directory, the coercive measures would have gone much further. In 1798, a proposal was put forward to make the wearing of the tricolor cockade compulsory, a measure which would have vastly increased the number of suspects. Then again, Sieyès advised the Directors to expel all the nobles from the Republic, a suggestion which was in accordance with what he had written in 1789: without them, the Third Estate would still remain the nation and indeed would be far better off as a result. The *sans-culottes* had often called for the general prescription of the enemy class, without the Committee of Public Safety ever agreeing to their demand. Sieyès now went further than the Committee; in advocating the most extreme measure of the Terror, he appears as the incarnation of the Revolutionary bourgeoisie, as fanatically opposed to the nobility as to democracy. La Revellière and Reubell protested indignantly, but Sieyès nonetheless got Boulay de la Meurthe to put forward his motion in the Five Hundred, on 3 Vendémiaire, Year VII (September 24, 1793): the nobles were to be denied citizenship unless they obtained naturalization under the same conditions as foreigners; exceptions would be made in the case of those who had rendered service to the Revolution; many nobles, on account of their offices or dignities under the *ancien régime*, would be exiled and their property liquidated, the proceeds being sent to them in the form of goods, after the deduction of an indemnity for the benefit of the nation. Feeling ran so high that Boulay declared on the twenty-ninth that he would not press the demand for exile. Although opposition continued, for example in the *Moniteur*, the deprivation of citizenship nonetheless became law on 9 Frimaire (November 29). However, for the law to be properly enforced, the Legislature would have had to indicate how exceptions were to be granted, and this it never did. Consequently the cases when it was applied to nobles seem to have been extremely rare.

The dry guillotine, as transportation to Guiana was called, left unpleasant memories, but the Directorial Terror was not particularly bloody, and above all—showing greater shrewdness than the Jacobin Terror—it aimed only at certain clearly defined categories. In reality, many of its measures served several purposes; the Directory could turn them against adversaries of every shade of opinion, and it did not fail to do so. However, the mass of the population never felt threatened as it had by the Law of Suspects. Moreover, the repression remained purely governmental; the Directory did not re-establish the revolutionary committees whose activity, all the more effective in that they possessed a detailed knowledge of local conditions, had opened the way to personal hatred and extortion and thus created irremediable divisions throughout the country. It should be added that in time a growing repugnance was shown for the harsher measures; no law was passed to aggravate the Terror until, in Year VII, the Royalists' collusion with France's enemies abroad reawakened the country's anger; after August, 1798, nobody left for Guiana, and after March, 1799, only one execution of an émigré was recorded.

If a Terror is indispensable to any dictatorship, it cannot make up for the incapacity of the rulers and for bad organization to insure effective government. The changes which had been effected in the ruling personnel of the Republic had not increased its value. Carnot and Barthélemy had been replaced by François de Neufchâteau, who had been looking after the Ministry of the Interior for six weeks, and Merlin de Douai, who left the Ministry of Justice. Of the Ministers of Year IV, only Ramel was left, and, as experience showed, the change had not been beneficial: only the Belgian jurist Lambrecht, who took the place of Merlin, was a man of any eminence. Moreover, the Executive, retaining its collective nature, remained exposed to internal disruption like the Committee of Public Safety. But the fundamental defect of the new dictatorship was that it left the Constitution as it was, without even suspending it as had been done in 1793.

This was not because the Directorials were all unaware of the distinction between the constitutional regime, which belongs to a time of internal and external peace, and the exceptional government, which extraordinary circumstances make it necessary to install in its place. On 19

Fructidor, the Directory itself had pointed out to the Ancients that "it was impossible to apply the ordinary rules to an extraordinary case unless one wanted to play into the enemy's hands"; Cabanis in Year VI, and Berlier in Year VII, argued forcefully that the constitutional guarantees could not be strictly observed as long as the Revolution had not been completed. The Monarchists had naturally protested indignantly at this relativity which the Montagnards had invoked to justify the Revolutionary government. Portalis had, however, mitigated the condemnation by adding that, if exceptional measures were necessary, they had to be provided for by the Constitution. But what if the latter was silent? And what if, as was the case, a delay of seven years was required before it could be revised? There was therefore no lack of people who argued that, since it had been violated on the eighteenth of Fructidor, it would be better to change it in order to give the dictatorship an appropriate organization. But, characteristically, the idea that occurred to one and all was not to introduce into the Constitution the possibility of suspending it wholly or partly for a time, after the manner of the Montagnards, but to effect a permanent transformation of the constituted powers in an authoritarian direction. Immediately after the *coup d'état*, there had been a rumor that the Directory was going to adjourn the Councils; it was denied. Soon afterwards, Boulay asked if it would not be advisable to institute a regular procedure in the event of conflict developing once more between the Directory and the Councils, a suggestion which was doubtless a hint that the Directory should be granted the right of dissolution. In November, Laussat, in the Ancients, called for a strengthening of the Executive. The Councils did not see things this way, but they envisaged an extension of their powers by the postponement of the elections. La Revellière tells how a delegation approached the Directory on the subject, and Barras adds that a similar approach was made in Ventôse, Year VI; according to this plan, only vacancies would have been filled, and the elections would have been put off for ten years. The most coherent projects seem to have been drawn up by Sieyès, with Talleyrand's help and probably also that of Madame de Staël and Benjamin Constant, who on several occasions praised Cromwell and Robespierre for having made the Executive preeminent. Lauraguais, one of Barras' relatives, kept him fully informed. Talleyrand told Bonaparte that Sieyès was proposing to go and see him, and we have the general's reply: he recommended depriving the Executive of the right to conclude peace or declare war, as well as the power to vote taxes! "The government's power, with all the latitude I give it, ought to be regarded as the real representative of the nation."

For the moment, nothing came of all this. The majority would have been quite willing to perpetuate itself, but had no intention of abdicating. The Directory, having had the *coup d'etat* legalized by the Councils, had not dared to ask them at the same time for a fresh increase in power. Besides, its members were not in agreement; La Revellière naïvely boasts of having maintained the Constitution by means of a trick, and his friend Daunou maintained that the eighteenth of Fructidor was "a purely conservative act." Reubell and Barras had no taste for these sophistries. But the former was suspicious of the latter, and even more so of Bonaparte. As for the economic organization which had enabled the Committee of Public Safety to maintain the currency and supply the armies, the Directorial bourgeoisie ruled it out as a matter of course, and, at a time when the armies were living on the conquered countries and the new political era seemed to promise a restoration of the nation's finances, it had no lack of arguments.

Therefore, no matter how much circumstances had increased the powers of the Directory, it remained defenseless in the face of the Councils and the Treasury. In the departments, administration remained unstable. But all the results of the eighteenth of Fructidor were going to be called in question—this was the essential point—by the annual elections, and, to begin with, no later than the following March.

At least it seemed for a few months that the unity of the Republicans had been restored. The declaration of ineligibility which the Convention had applied to some of the Montagnards was repealed. The Directory once again included a good many Jacobins in its appointments and took care not to offend their papers. A few legislative measures were taken to please them. The Santo Domingo elections having been validated, Sonthonax took his seat, while the law on the return of the settlers was annulled. Plans were made for a reform of the judiciary, in view of the constant denunciations of the partiality of the courts. There was no fixed term for the electoral mandate of the judges, prosecutors and clerks of the criminal courts: a law remedied this defect and entrusted the Directory with the task of finding replacements for those who had been elected in Year IV. Another law provided for revision of the list of jurors in those departments where the elections had been annulled. What the Jacobins wanted most of all was for a process of reconsideration to be made available to Republicans who had reason to complain of Royalist judges: the Directory took a favorable view of this request, but the Councils considered that it would be difficult to produce a legal definition of a reasonable claim, and pointed out that criminals might take advantage of the provisions. Distrust of the terrorists came to the surface now and then. The apologists of the eighteenth of Fructidor never spared them their invective. When Lamarque obtained for the acquitted terrorists of Vendôme the indemnity laid down by a law of the Convention, the Ancients rejected the resolution. In Frimaire, Rabaut expressed alarm at the Directory's Jacobin appointments.

However, until the end of the winter, the Directory did not seem to suspect that the danger lay with the Left, and there is reason to believe that it was chiefly preoccupied with the generals. Augereau had been given command of the armies of the Sambre and Meuse and of the Rhine and Moselle, joined together under the name of the Army of Germany; he complained loudly of ingratitude, for he wanted a place in the Directory; soon it was alleged that he was plotting with the Jacobins of Strasbourg, and he was sent to the Pyrenees under the pretext of preparing an expedition against Portugal. Bonaparte, after playing a double game, was irritated that the eighteenth of Fructidor had not opened the gates of power to him; the Directory had been obliged to send him Botot, Barras' secretary, and to let him arrange the Treaty of Campo-Formio as he wished, so eager did he seem to throw in his hand. From Italy he went by way of Switzerland to Rastatt, to open negotiations with the Empire, and then went to Paris, where he was solemnly received on 20 Frimaire, Year VI (December 10, 1797). His attitude was cold and haughty;

in reply to Barras' speech he made the famous comment: "When the happiness of the French people is based on better organic laws, the whole of Europe will become free." During the following months, he was nonetheless consulted on foreign affairs, and, more than anyone else, he got the Republic to bog itself down in the path which he had done so much to make it take.

CHAPTER NINE

The War Against England and the Resumption of Propaganda

At Campo-Formio, France had made peace with the great Continental powers; but the war against England was still going on, and since 1793 this duel had caused her considerable harm. Compelled to conquer on land if she were not to perish, she had, as past experience should have enabled her to foresee, been obliged to give up ruling the seas, or at the very least maintaining a balance of power at sea—all the more so in that the emigration of officers, indiscipline, the shortage of money and the treachery of

Toulon had ruined her navy. After the 1793 campaign, England on the contrary had neglected the Continent where she did not reappear until 1799; confining herself to keeping the struggle going with her subsidies, she had devoted the greater part of her resources to naval and colonial warfare. The French squadrons hardly ever left port; true, the British blockade was frequently interrupted, especially in winter, but even so they moved about only stealthily and did not look for a fight. The shipowners, as usual, had fitted out privateers from which great things were expected; but the English, grouping their merchant ships together in escorted convoys, were less and less afraid of commerce being destroyed, whereas France's shipping trade was gradually wasting away.

Separated from her colonies, she had seen most of them fall into the enemy's hands or break away from her. At Santo Domingo, after Sonthonax had been recalled, General Laveaux, keeping only a few towns in the north of the island, had rallied to his cause Toussaint L'Ouverture, one of the Negro leaders, who, with the help of Rivaud, a mulatto who had held out in the south, had fairly quickly forced the English to evacuate the island. But it was not long before he made himself master of the colony; Laveaux and Sonthonax, returning on mission, were sent back to France under the pretext that they had been elected deputies; while General Hédouville, who replaced them, would soon leave in his turn. Toussaint, who incidentally displayed a truly statesmanlike genius, did not break with the Directory, but the authority of the mother country was no longer anything but nominal. In Guadeloupe, Victor Hugues, who had reconquered the island in 1794, was managing to hold out; the other West Indian islands—Tobago,

Saint Lucia and Martinique—were lost; the same was true of Dutch Guiana and of Trinidad, which belonged to Spain. The French islands in the Indian Ocean were still safe, but the Île de France, refusing to abolish slavery, had forced the Directory's commissioners to re-embark.

It was the West Indies which supplied France with most of the colonial produce—especially sugar—which she distributed to her neighbors; her trade could not make good the loss of them and, as for the rest, while peace on the Continent reopened markets to it, it could not benefit greatly from them without maritime transport. Its fate therefore depended to a large extent on the help which it could obtain from neutral shipping, which in turn depended on the British blockade. The English refused to allow neutral flags to cover enemy merchandise, and, in order to seize that merchandise as well as contraband of war, arrogated to themselves the right of search on the high seas. In reality, they granted all sorts of licenses which considerably attenuated the harshness of these rules, because they were aimed much less at ruining the enemy's military power than at enabling the English merchants to earn money in his place. From this point of view, there was no objection to even selling to the enemy in order to obtain his currency; the blockade was mercantile rather than warlike. The neutral ships were indispensable to traffic with the enemy; besides, English trade was too considerable to do without them, and political considerations often led to the making of concessions. They were therefore given licenses on condition that they came into an English port to have their cargo inspected and to pay taxes. They protested in the name of "the freedom of the seas," but one and all—Hanseatics, Scandinavians and

Americans—submitted, especially since they were making large profits. The disputes were above all concerned with colonial produce. In peacetime, France, like the other powers, reserved trade with her colonies for herself, but when at war with England, being unable to reach them, she suspended her exclusive rights and opened their ports to neutrals. England forbade the latter to take advantage of this permission, and reserved the trade with the enemy colonies for her own shipping. On this point too, a compromise had been reached: in 1794, after the United States had agreed to close their ports to the French privateers, they were allowed in exchange to import and re-export French colonial produce; the European neutrals had been given permission to go and fetch that produce to ship it either to their own ports or to England.

During the American War, France had respected the freedom of the neutrals, and the latter asked for nothing better than to help her as far as British controls would allow. But the Convention, adopting a policy of reprisals, had applied the same principles as the English, and thus harmed the neutrals; under the influence of the protectionists, it had even forbidden the admission of English merchandise and passed a "navigation act" forbidding foreign ships to bring anything into France except produce from their own countries. In fact, finding it impossible to do without the neutrals, the Committee of Public Safety had quickly returned to an opportunist policy similar to that of the English, and the Thermidorians had followed this by reviving the treaties of trade and navigation. All the same, the ban on British merchandise remained, and on 10 Brumaire, Year V (October 30, 1796), it had been aggravated by a law which branded a great many goods as English, whatever their real source, and for the rest called for the production of a certificate of origin issued by the appropriate consul. Domiciliary visits had followed and, as in 1793, British subjects had even been arrested. In the course of the following summer, the Directory informed the neutral countries that it would seize their ships, even on the high seas, if they continued to comply with England's requirements. However, until the eighteenth of Fructidor, it does not seem that in practice they ceased to place themselves at the service of French trade. Theoretically, France had done everything to make the English blockade as impervious as possible to the enemy's will, but the need to export and to obtain certain raw materials had likewise forced her to make certain concessions.

Confronted by these results of the English war, thoughtful Frenchmen, however preoccupied they might be with hostilities on the Continent, were obliged to admit that France and England had probably arrived at the last act of the "Second Hundred Years' War," begun under Louis XIV for the control of the high seas and of the world. Most of their compatriots, being countrymen, did not bother their heads very much about such problems, but they hated the English as traditional enemies and accused "perfidious Albion" of having taken the lead of the counter-revolutionary crusade, and having subsidized the Coalition, in order to satisfy her selfish greed with impunity. They did not believe her to be invincible for a moment. At that time of wooden sailing-ships, coal and iron had not yet given the English that superiority which would make competition impossible; and seaboard conscription was a better source of recruits than the press-gang. Then again, England had no national army and employed only merce-

naries; while there could be no question of sending Republican troops to conquer India or the West Indies, the idea
of landing them in England did not seem impossible, nor
did that of winning over Ireland, which was always ready
to rise in revolt; an attempt made in December 1796 had
failed, but that had been due to a storm and not to the
enemy fleet. The economic war too, right from the start,
had seemed full of promise. For the French the strength
of a State lay essentially in its peasants and its agriculture;
the state of production, the influence of the Physiocrats,
and the example of the Roman Republic—all combined
to fill them with contempt for the modern Carthage
whose life depended on an export trade built on the arti-
ficial and fragile scaffolding of credit. She had only to be
prevented from trading with the Continent and she would
be reduced to bankruptcy, starvation, and revolution.

When the eighteenth of Fructidor reawakened the old
revolutionary ardor, it was therefore not simply the spirit
of propaganda which it benefited: the conclusion of peace
on the Continent also enabled it to turn against England,
all the more so in that the alliances with Spain and Holland inspired boundless hopes. In a circular of Nivôse,
Year VI, Talleyrand—the Anglophile!—inveighed against
the tyrants of the world, the vampires of the sea, which the
Republic was going to exterminate for the benefit of civ-
ilization and in order to liberate the oppressed nations,
thus earning the latter's undying gratitude. These bellicose
accents undoubtedly awakened a response; The Directory
was able to float a loan of eighty million francs, and inventors came forward with proposals for dirigible balloons
and even submarines. The Irish, who had risen in revolt in
1798, had been crushed; nonetheless, an invasion of Eng-

land was decided on. About fifty thousand men were moved to Brest, and Bonaparte was given command of the "Army of England"; he seems to have taken the plan seriously for a while. At the same time, the economic war took on a new character. On 29 Nivôse, Year VI (January 18, 1798), a law putting the Directory's threats into effect made it possible to seize those neutral ships which had complied with English requirements or on which any article of British origin was found, even if it were only a sailor's knife or the captain's cutlery. This harshness seemed incredible; it increased the number of prizes, the privateers enthusiastically making themselves the instruments of the law. The merchants who saw the neutrals deserting the French ports, and the consumers who were deprived of colonial produce, protested, but so also did the manufacturers: this was not how they understood protection. They were quite willing to have a ban on manufactured goods which competed with their own, but they wanted to receive the raw material they lacked, especially cotton: and they approved of the "Continental blockade" —for the Napoleonic method would be nothing else— provided it remained mercantile like the British blockade, and did not become warlike at their expense. In the event, exceptions to the law of 10 Brumaire, Year V, had to be made in the case of tools, agricultural implements, and calico intended for printing. And at bottom, the Directory really considered that a policy of opportunism remained necessary: it asked the Councils to restore its jurisdiction over prizes of war, unwisely transferred to the ordinary courts, so that it could regulate the enforcement of the blockade to suit the complicated interests of the Republic.

Even so, the policy which had been adopted seriously

weakened French exports and had a deplorable influence on external relations. The United States jibbed and took retaliatory measures against French shipping, so that the two republics found themselves practically in a state of war. However, the Americans agreed to negotiate, and Talleyrand took the opportunity to ask their envoys for a jug of wine; when the latter's correspondence was communicated to the Senate and made public in the spring of 1798, a terrible scandal resulted. Then again, the economic war, interpreted in this way, could not have its full effect except if the whole Continent co-operated, a state of affairs which could only push France into the policy of conquest already encouraged by the spirit of propaganda. The completion of the conquest of Italy and the seizure of the Hanseatic ports and Hanover, in order to close Germany to English trade, were consequences which naturally recommended themselves to the advocates of total war. The annexation of Mülhausen and Geneva took place in 1798; it can be explained, at least in part, by the desire to suppress two centers of smuggling.

Alone now in face of a bigger and threatening France, England became aware of her perilous position, and the war, for her, began to become a national affair. The preparations for an invasion, however, were soon abandoned. From Holland and Spain the Directory obtained nothing. In 1797 Jervis had beaten the Spaniards off Cape St. Vincent; he blockaded Cádiz, and Nelson's squadron entered the Mediterranean; Brueys declared that he was incapable of bringing the Corfu squadron to Brest; Duncan routed the Dutch at Camperduyn. The military leaders were skeptical about the chances of success. On 5 Ventôse, Year VI (February 23, 1798), on his return from an inspection in the west, Bonaparte decided to abandon the project. It had no other consequences but the dispatch, in August, of a small expeditionary force to Ireland: General Humbert succeeded in landing, but was soon surrounded and had to surrender.

There had been no lack of reasons to justify the abandonment of the scheme: the navy could not guarantee the crossing, and, moreover, the Republic was not sufficiently sure of peace on the Continent to deprive itself of an excellent army and its best general. But Bonaparte had added that, if negotiations for peace were not opened with England, the war had to be taken to Egypt, and there was not a single one of the arguments against the invasion of England which did not apply, with even greater force, to this new undertaking; there were also several others which condemned it in its own right.

That Bonaparte's imagination should have flown after Alexander toward an almost legendary Orient was only to be expected after the occupation of the Ionian Isles, the expression of his views on Malta, and the dispatch of an agent to Ali-Tebelen, the Pasha of Janina; nothing could be less surprising. He would certainly have preferred to conquer England, if that had proved possible. As soon as that plan had to be given up, the Orient returned to the foreground. For Bonaparte could not remain idle without running the risk of compromising himself in political intrigues which were still premature, and without peace dimming his prestige. If his choice fell on Egypt, that was probably due to Talleyrand, and there is some mystery about the part played by the latter. True, Egypt had occupied a place in French tradition since the Crusades, and in the trade of Marseilles since the Capitulations; the mer-

chants had been complaining for years about the Mamelukes, the mercenaries who exploited the country under
the nominal authority of the Sultan; and the consul
Magallon maintained that an invasion would be sure to
succeed. Egypt, moreover, was on the way to India,
where Tippoo was still defending Maisur against Welles-
ley. In Messidor, Year V, speaking to the Institute, Talleyrand had advocated the resumption of colonial expansion,
and Egypt was one of the most splendid preys anyone
could wish for. But it could not escape Talleyrand's notice
that an agreement with England, which he had always
wanted, would be impossible if, while insisting on keeping
the natural frontiers whose acquisition he himself approved
—even though his admirers have suggested the contrary—
the Republic also undertook an overseas conquest that
might alarm its rival; and none was more calculated to do
so than that of Egypt. Then again, one of the principles
of the Republic's policy had been to abstain from any intervention in eastern Europe, and it was by keeping silent
on the Polish partitions that it had been able to detach
Prussia from the Coalition. By conquering Egypt, on the
other hand, it risked provoking war with Turkey, for it was
in vain that Talleyrand maintained that the Sultan did not
care about such an illusory possession; worse still, it meant
reopening the Eastern question without the consent of Rus-
sia, thus arousing her enmity and inciting her to fight the
French, which was something she had always avoided. Talleyrand was closely associated with Bonaparte; was he
simply trying here to serve him to the detriment of the
nation? That is possible. But, since he was in the habit of
selling himself to the highest bidder, it has been suggested
that he might have undertaken to divert toward Egypt the

army that was threatening England with invasion, and to provoke the formation of a new Coalition, as he would against Napoleon. The Directory had reason to suspect him: a letter from Madame Grand, his mistress, to a London correspondent, maintaining that Piedcourt (Talleyrand suffered from a club foot) wanted to "help his English friends," had been intercepted; the lady was arrested and then released. It must be assumed that, on the eve of the dreaded elections of Year VI, the Directory considered it out of the question to force Bonaparte and Talleyrand into opposition; but that it should have adopted their rash proposal for a reason of that sort tells heavily against it.

Even if it had rejected the plan of an invasion of Egypt, peace on the Continent would still have been necessary if it was to wage war on England with any chance of success. Everything, however, simultaneously impelled the Directory toward a policy of invasion which could only compromise peace: the influence of the generals and the contractors, the revolutionary ardor which it itself shared, the vague desire to deprive England of her markets in order to monopolize them, and even the temptation to secure all possible guarantees in anticipation of a new war. The enslavement of the sister republics soon became obvious. It was important that Batavia should have a stable government, capable of helping her protector, and this was far from being the case. True, the provisional rulers, who had been in power since 1795, had submitted a constitution for popular ratification in August, 1797, but a coalition of the supporters of the House of Orange and the unitarian democrats had rejected it. After the eighteenth of Fructidor, Delacroix, the French envoy to The Hague, came to an agreement with the latter to propose a *coup d'état* to Paris.

Daëndels, who was in command of the Dutch army, and Joubert, the commander of the occupation forces, had promised their co-operation. On 3 Pluviôse, Year VI (January 22, 1798), the Batavian Assembly declared itself to be a constituent body, and, after purging itself, drew up a new constitution which, this time, was accepted. It was just as necessary to make sure of the Cisalpine Republic. On 3 Ventôse (February 21), the Directory concluded a treaty of alliance with it which prolonged the occupation of the country by a force of twenty-five thousand men at the expense of the new republic; at the same time a liberal trade agreement was signed, but this did not prevent the Cisalpine Councils from rejecting both treaty and agreement, as impossibly onerous. The regime in power had been instituted by Bonaparte without either popular ratification or French approval; the Directory therefore considered itself as much at liberty to intervene and change it as it had been in Holland. The Councils were purged and arrests carried out, after which the treaties were ratified.

Bonaparte's conquest, incidentally, was the parade-ground of the advocates of propaganda, and it was chiefly around the Cisalpine Republic that the latter exerted their influence. There, coming from all parts of Italy, and joining up with the generals and the contractors, there gathered all those who dreamed of turning the peninsula into a unitarian republic. The Cisalpine conservatives themselves considered that in return for the alliance with France their country should be enlarged at the expense of the Pope and Piedmont. Cisalpine bands kept entering the Marches and it was hoped that in Rome the revolutionaries would take action. They did in fact start a riot on December 28, 1797, but their adversaries got the upper hand and, holding the

French responsible, threatened the Embassy, which was
then under Joseph Bonaparte; in the brawl that followed,
General Duphot was killed. The Directory's hostility towards the Papacy was too fierce for it to miss the opportunity. Berthier, who was now in command of the Army of
Italy, received orders to march on Rome, and Bonaparte
encouraged him. However, the Directory had no intention of
letting the Roman Republic become a new Cisalpine Republic for Berthier, and it immediately sent a Civil Commission to organize it, which was joined by Daunou and
Monge. Berthier, in any case, found the task he had been
given repugnant. Arriving outside Rome on 11 February,
he was nonplused when Pius VI accepted all his conditions;
the revolutionaries having proclaimed a republic in the
Forum, in the midst of a crowd of onlookers, and called in
the French, he occupied the city, sent the Pope off to
Sienna, and let Masséna take over. The Commission proclaimed a constitution, drawn up by Merlin, which, until
the end of hostilities, submitted the laws and the actions
of the "consuls" to the ratification of the French general,
so that the Roman Republic immediately became the
least free of them all. It was also the most heavily ran-
somed: Haller, the contractors, and the generals had started
looting right from the beginning. The junior officers protested indignantly and, when Masséna arrived, mutinied;
this general was reputed to be one of the boldest of looters
and they bore him a long-standing grudge, since most of
them belonged to the regiments which Moreau had sent to
Bonaparte, under Bernadotte's command, at the beginning
of 1797, and which had come to blows with his division.
The Commission was unable to restore order, and finally
the Directory was obliged to appoint a new commander:

Gouvion-Saint-Cyr, one of Moreau's lieutenants. The Roman Republic thus began under the most unfavorable auspices.

It was from Bonaparte, determined to join the Cisalpine Republic to France by way of Valais, that the decisive impulse came which led to the creation of the Helvetian Republic. Switzerland was then only a confederation of independent cantons, governed by privileged bourgeois patriciates which, having gained control over some part of the country, treated the inhabitants as subjects: this is how the Vaud region had become a sort of Bernese colony. The Swiss patriots, notably Ochs of Basle, wanted both to create a unitarian republic of which every Swiss would be a citizen, and to overthrow the oligarchy. Unwilling to count on an insurrection, they hoped that France, without occupying Switzerland, would behave in a sufficiently threatening way for the oligarchy to collapse. The Directory had no lack of grievances against the latter, but it had secured the expulsion of Mallet du Pan, Wickham and the émigrés; an agreement was under consideration giving France the Jura territories and the town of Bienne; these she claimed as dependencies of the bishopric of Basle, which had become the department of Mont-Terrible. So far, the suggestions of the Swiss democrats had not met with any response, any more than the claims made by Laharpe, a native of Vaud—claims based on a sixteenth-century treaty by which France, while recognizing the rights of Berne over the Vaud region, had nonetheless guaranteed the latter's liberties. The affair was set in motion on December 8, 1797, at a dinner at Reubell's which brought together Bonaparte and Ochs. Soon afterwards, Ochs began a campaign to get the cantons to accept a constitution

drawn up by Merlin and Reubell. Several cantons gave their
assent. At the same time, a division of the Army of Italy had
been moved to the frontier of the Vaud region, though with
orders not to cross the border unless it was attacked. But
as the inhabitants of Vaud had lost no time in giving their
support to the new constitution, the Bernese sent a few
troops to attack them: the French commander despatched
an envoy to parley with them, and in the darkness he was
fired at by mistake; the Vaud region was immediately occupied. So far the situation was not irremediable. All of a
sudden, in the night of February 13-14, 1798, the Directory
ordered its troops to march on Berne, probably at Bonaparte's suggestion. Brune advanced from Lausanne, and
Schauenbourg from the Jura; the town was occupied after
some fairly severe fighting. The Directory immediately appointed a civil commissioner, a former member of the Convention called Lecarlier, who was given Rapinat, Reubell's
brother-in-law, as his assistant. They enforced the constitution, seized the Treasury of Berne, imposed a levy of fifteen
million francs on the cantons, and tried to put an end to
arbitrary requisitioning and looting; but they had to put
down the insurrection of the highlanders of Schwytz, Uri
and Unterwald, as well as that of Valais. The Bernese,
showing greater cunning, bribed Talleyrand and obtained a
treaty which reduced their levy. Lecarlier, who had been
appointed Minister of Police, had just been succeeded by
Rapinat, who flew into a rage and refused to enforce this
treaty, thus incurring the wrath of the Swiss Directory: on
28 Prairial (June 17), without consulting Paris, he carried
out a *coup d'état* which broke all resistance. The Helvetian
Republic was not beginning very much better than the
Roman Republic.

Piedmont only narrowly escaped the same fate. In 1797, the King of Sardinia had ruthlessly repressed a revolutionary movement, and, after the eighteenth of Fructidor, had lost no time in ratifying the treaty of alliance with France which until then he had left in abeyance. However, Cisalpines and Genoese were impatient to extend their territories at his expense. The representative of France, Ginguené, had no sooner arrived at Turin than he set about helping them, and Brune, appointed commander of the Army of Italy, allied himself with the Jacobins in Milan; soon afterwards, armed bands entered Piedmont. For months, the Directory posed as a mediator; finally, after Ginguené had succeeded, on 9 Messidor (June 27), in imposing on the terrified King a convention which handed over the citadel of Turin to the French, it thought fit to keep this prize.

Austria could scarcely have been expected to view this extension of French influence with equanimity. Not that Thugut expressed any indignation at it; still looking for an opportunity of self-aggrandizement in Italy, he simply bided his time. At Campo-Formio, it had been agreed that, if France made fresh acquisitions, Austria would be entitled to compensation. It is true that the Roman and Helvetian Republics were supposed to be independent. But at Rastatt, the Directory exceeded the provisions of the Treaty of Campo-Formio. Reubell regretted that the Cologne region should have been left to the Empire, and, from the point of view of general policy, the Directory could not give up its claims to that region without alienating Prussia which, ceding nothing more, would not be entitled to any of the annexations she was planning in Germany; this was playing into the hands of Austria, which had in fact wanted to foil her rival. Consequently Treilhard, who had taken

Bonaparte's place at the Congress, demanded the whole of the left bank of the Rhine and obtained a general agreement from the Diet on 19 Ventôse (March 9). Cobenzl immediately asked for compensation. Treilhard's retort was as surprising as it was categorical: the Cologne region, having been under military occupation for a long time, could not be regarded as a new acquisition. In these circumstances, war was in sight. It seemed imminent when, in April, Bernadotte, the French Ambassador in Vienna, was attacked by rioters after hoisting the tricolor flag, and, failing to obtain suitable redress, left the city.

However, it was postponed. Neither Thugut, who was not ready, nor the Directory, which was preoccupied with the current elections, was prepared to begin hostilities. Moreover, the wind had changed once again in Paris: the Directory had just broken with the Jacobins, and for a moment it seemed likely that its foreign policy would be modified as a result.

CHAPTER TEN

The New Anti-Jacobin Reaction; the Twenty-Second of Floréal, Year VI (May 11, 1798)

After the eighteenth of Fructidor, the elections of Year VI had soon become the major preoccupation of the Directory and the Councils. A great deal was at stake, for what was involved was not strictly speaking a partial change of representatives, since the recent exclusions had greatly increased the number of unforeseen vacancies: there were 437 deputies to be elected. The disappearance of the last third of the "perpetual" members of the Convention made the situation still more serious. Until Pluviôse, the Royalist peril remained the overriding problem. Since the suspension of the elections had not been agreed, the Directory resorted to other expedients, which were no less contrary to the spirit of representative government and which, for that reason, had been rejected in Year V. The law of 12 Pluviôse, Year VI (January 31, 1798) charged the existing Legislature with the task of checking the credentials of the newly elected deputies; thus the outgoing deputies would purge their successors! Another law, that of 24 Pluviôse (February 12), stipulated that the election of the new Directory should take place on 27 Floréal (May 16), a measure which likewise allocated it to the existing Legislature: whatever the new majority might be, the Directory would nonetheless remain entirely Republican.

Gradually, however, it became apparent that not many Royalists would vote in the elections: the new Terror would intimidate them. Some of them advocated abstention, the law of 19 Fructidor having imposed upon the electors the oath of hatred for the Monarchy; many of them would be excluded by the law of 3 Brumaire, Year IV, and the one which had just been passed against the nobles; in Ventôse, yet another law excluded all those who had rendered services to the rebels. Nobody could have any illusions about the prestige of the Directory and its minions. Was there not reason to believe, therefore, that the effacement of the Royalists would benefit the Jacobins most of all? In the provinces, the Constitutional Clubs were chiefly directed by them and, thanks to the new appointments, there was no lack of administrators and commissioners to favor them. In Côte-d'Or there were nine clubs, and in the Sarthe twenty-five. The Le Mans club organized what was known as an *ambulance* or perambulation: every tenth day, it went in procession to the seat of some canton where colleagues and friends had prepared a fête, concluding with the foundation of a new club which in its turn propagated itself in the neighboring communes. The ban on affiliations could not prevent them from acting together. The result was a ready-made election "machine."

But apart from this propaganda, it may be that the proposals made by Pons de Verdun in the Five Hundred, on 22 Nivôse (January 8) and again on 3 Ventôse (February 24) greatly contributed to shifting the danger back to the Left in the eyes of the Directorials. To take part in the primary assemblies which opened on 1 Germinal, it was necessary, according to the Constitution, to have one year's residence, dating from inscription on the civic register; in Year V, the Republican majority had realized that, the previous year, its supporters had been unable to demand or obtain inscription on account of the White Terror, and it had decided that all who entered their names up to 30 Ventôse should be deemed to have done so a year before. Adopted only five days before 1 Germinal, this measure had had no effect. Pons asked for it to be revived. As it was bound to benefit the Jacobins most of all, it is significant that the Ancients should have rejected, on two occasions in Year VI, a resolution which had struck them as legitimate in Year V. Pons also wanted favorable consideration to be given until 30 Ventôse to those citizens who offered to pay the tax of three days' work in order to become eligible to vote. Again it is significant that Régnier should have cried: "Anybody would think that Pons regarded as good Republicans precisely those people who don't pay taxes"; and that Pilastre, one of La Revellière's friends, should have protested that in Year V there had probably not been as many as fifty men in the whole of France who had acquired the right to vote in that way. To understand the rejection of Pons' proposal, it is sufficient to recall that the Constitution restricted voluntary registration to the month of Messidor, and the full meaning of these acrimonious remarks becomes apparent: Pons had annoyed the Directorials with an ingenuous movement in the direction of universal suffrage. Thus, at the very moment when laws were directed against the Royalists, an anti-Jacobin reaction began which was to turn them to its own purpose.

La Revellière was thoroughly alarmed, for he had been warned that terrorists were planning to assassinate him during the walk that he took nearly every day to the Jardin des Plantes, to see his friend the botanist Thouin. Merlin, for his part, out of fear too or as a deliberate policy, revived Carnot's role with the same stubborn hatred for those whose views he had represented in 1793. Once again, the Directory repeated the accusation, which, in Year II, had enabled the Committee of Public Safety to crush simultaneously the extremists of both Right and Left: it denounced both branches of the counterrevolutionary conspiracy, that of the White Cockade and that of the Red Cap. In point of fact, there was no danger that the electors would choose terrorists, but by confusing the democrats with them, the Directory was sure of creating an impression, for what the bourgeoisie dreaded was not only the Terror but also the social democracy of Year II. "Social fear" was therefore a valuable help to the Directory. The *Moniteur* alarmed landowners by reporting "posters in which shameless anarchists preached the leveling-down and the equality of Robespierre; and promised to give those who have not, the property of those who have." On 9 Ventôse (February 27), at the Constitutional Club, Benjamin Constant called on property owners to rally to the Directory:

The Revolution was carried out to insure liberty and equality for all while leaving the property of each inviolate. It has therefore undertaken to defend that property . . . ; all the government's powers, all the legislators' measures must aim at maintaining it, consolidating it, surrounding it with a sacred barrier.

In reality, those who have been called the Neo-Jacobins were not communists any more than they were terrorists, but it is true that they were quite capable of partially reviving the social democracy of Year II, and this was what had to be avoided at all costs. "Whoever outlaws wealth conspires against mediocrity," added Constant. Well said!

It was in vain that Barras protested at the division which was going to be created once more among the Republicans, for his colleagues had ulterior motives. For Reubell—and probably also for Merlin, who was no less authoritarian—the main object was not so much to exclude the democrats as to provide the Directory with a docile majority. In spite of the solidarity of the Fructidorians, the Councils' hidden jealousy of the Executive had been awakened a good many times. Lamarque had deplored the fact that the legislators should be "so to speak effaced from the political body." Since the Directory had annulled the lists of jurors drawn up by the central administrations it dismissed, the legality of its decrees had once more been disputed. It had been refused the right of dismissal with respect to the judges, prosecutors, and clerks of the criminal courts. It had also been refused control over the theaters. In the course of financial debates, criticism was beginning to be made of government extravagance. La Revellière claims, incidentally—and this is quite probable—that Chénier, Baudin, Camus and many others had gone into opposition because they had not obtained the privileges or the consideration to which they felt they were entitled, and that all the deputies were annoyed at having no influence in the ministerial offices. Nothing illustrates this conflict better than the affair of the cloaks. The Constitution prescribed for the deputies, as for the Directors, an official uniform and, in January 1798, this uniform was being made in Lyons when the police of that city confiscated the material as being of English origin. A storm of indignation broke out in the Councils at this attack on the majesty of national representation, and a law was passed requiring the Directory to order the restitution of the material. The government saw that, if the Fructidorians showed little gratitude to it, the future majority might be even less docile. One can therefore form only an imperfect idea of its intentions and the resulting consequences if one imagines that the Jacobins, such as Dubois-Crancé or General Jourdan, were the only ones to cause it concern; it was no less anxious to outlaw independents such as Lamarque, a former Girondin. Apart from the fact that every government is naturally drawn to a policy of this sort, it was bound to recommend itself once the Directory had returned to a dictatorship without suspending elections. The Committee of Public Safety had broken all resistance in the Convention, and Bonaparte, as First Consul, would declare bluntly: "There must be no opposition."

Having made up its mind, the Directory prepared for the elections with much greater care than in Year V; besides, this time it had a much wider range of means at its disposal. Merlin increased the number of dismissals; first of all, Sotin, Minister of Police of the eighteenth of Fructidor, suspected of Jacobinism, was replaced by Dondeau, one of this Director's tools. Envoys were sent out to spur on the commissioners in secret: for this purpose, inspectors were used whose official function was to supervise the enforcement, now begun at last, of the highway toll; they were provided with funds, and also with a list of the candidates approved by the Directory. Intimidation was also used: certain administrations and commissioners carried out arrests of suspects; Lyons, Marseilles and several other towns were placed under martial law. But Merlin's favorite expedient, one very characteristic of his crafty mind, was to turn the law of 12 Pluviôse against his adversaries, by systematically organizing secessions which would enable the present majority to validate whomsoever it pleased. These secessions were therefore a common feature of the elections of Year VI. In Paris, for example, the electoral assembly of the Oratoire, which was almost entirely left-wing, saw Merlin's confederates withdraw to the Institut, where they finally gathered together 212 electors out of 609. These maneuvers were not always successful. In the Sarthe, the Central Administration fought only the Royalists, and allowed the clubs' delegates to hold a meeting on 5 Ventôse (March 5) to draw up the list of candidates; the same day, the Directory suppressed the clubs and their newspaper, and dismissed three members of the Central Administration as well as several other officials. The left-wing list nonetheless went through unaltered. However, the fact remains that a majority of Directorials was elected; but, in order to obtain the exclusion of the opponents it feared, the Directory was obliged to terrorize the population, and the elections were said to have been execrable.

The Councils set to work checking them in accordance with the regular procedure; this operation was not expected to be completed before 1 Prairial, in which case the deputies who had not been invalidated would take their seats. In order to exclude the "wild beasts," as Creuzé-Latouche called them, it was suggested before long that the method should be changed; Régnier asked that the "brave seceders" be encouraged. Lamarque defended the majority principle: the Directory's confidants retorted that, first of all, since the electors had taken an oath of hatred for the Monarchy and the Constitution of 1793, they could not have elected Royalists or Jacobins without perjuring themselves, in which case the election was null and void; and that secondly, in order to exclude unworthy persons, the Legislature had an implicit right of censure over the newly elected deputies, a right which was justified chiefly by examples taken from the United States. When a message was sent to the Directory asking for any information it might have, the Left did not fail to point out that this would enable it to dictate a choice of deputies, so that the deviation from the majority principle would end up by giving the government power to purge the Legislature, a state of affairs which was the negation of the representative system.

On 13 Floréal (May 2), the Directory replied by denouncing the conspiracy of the Royalists and the Anarchists, and, on the fifteenth, the Five Hundred, after validating the elections made at the Institut for the department of the Seine, suspended the operation. As far as the majority was concerned, that was the end of the matter. Its leaders, Bailleul and Hardy, joined with the Directors to draw up a hurried list of exclusions, and, on the eighteenth, asked the Council to adopt it *en bloc*. General Jourdan made an eloquent protest, asking for each item to be examined and voted upon separately, but his adversaries urged the hesitant Assembly to bar the way to the Terror. "The guillotine is ready," Crassous is alleged to have said, according to Barras; "do you want to mount the scaffold?" The reply went without saying. The Ancients ratified the list without turning a hair.

The law of 22 Floréal, Year VI (May 11, 1798) validated the elections in forty-seven departments out of ninety-six. It excluded the deputies in eight departments where there had been secession, so that their seats remained vacant; in nineteen others, the seceders were preferred on account of their political color. Elsewhere, one or more representatives were disqualified; what is more, over sixty administrators or judges were set aside. Altogether, 106 deputies were expelled, including Lamarque himself; about sixty members of the opposition seem to have escaped. The elections did not by any means present the threatening appearance they were alleged to have, but the majority loyal to the Directors had no doubt been reduced, and, if the minority had not been left without leadership, it might well have embarrassed them. The governmental character of the *journée* becomes even more obvious when it is realized that sixty-eight commissioners and seventeen other officials nominated by the Directory figured among those admitted, as well as 106 administrators and judges, many of whom it had probably also chosen, so that over 150 deputies had used their official positions to impose themselves on the electors and could be regarded as government agents. Although the twenty-second of Floréal seems to have run counter to the eighteenth of Fructidor, it confirmed the latter by aggravating that subjection of the Legislature which was to be one of the essential features of the Napoleonic regime. The intrusion of government officials would indeed vitiate the representative system until 1848.

A few measures followed for the benefit of the Executive; it was given authority to fill any vacancies in the ranks of the judges, prosecutors and clerks of the criminal courts until Year VII, and similar authority with respect to the magistrates elected in Year V. As for the change in the personnel of the Directory, it took place on 27 Floréal, in accordance with the law of 24 Pluviôse: the place of François de Neufchâteau was taken by the jurist Treilhard, a regicide and former member of the Constituent Assembly. He had left the Legislature on 1 Prairial, Year IV, and it could therefore be argued that he was not eligible, but in Ventôse it had been maintained that the interval of one year had to be counted from the resignation from office to the return to office and not to the election, without anybody raising any objection. Treilhard's accession did nothing to enhance the prestige of the Directory, for it meant yet another lawyer to sit with "King" Barras—an arrogant lawyer, what is more, who would soon increase the number of malcontents.

The Directorials were well aware that, having broken the unity of the Republicans, they ran the risk of seeing the Royalists raise their heads again. To guard against this danger, they authorized on 18 Messidor (July 6) domiciliary visits for a period of one month, incidentally without much result, and they took active measures against those citizens liable to deportation who had so far escaped; the law of 19 Brumaire, Year VII (November 9, 1798) made it possible to inscribe those who did not give themselves up on the list of émigrés. In point of fact, most of the trouble suffered by the

Directory came from the Jacobins and its own majority. On 26 Prairial, Year VI (June 17, 1798), a banquet which brought the deputies together at the Hôtel Biron ended in uproar, some of the guests having refused to drink the health of the new Directory. As for the majority, dissatisfied with itself for having excluded a good many men it esteemed, it was also dissatisfied with the government which had forced it to give way. It is significant that on several occasions the Presidents were taken from the Left: Pérès de la Haute-Garonne, Savary, General Jourdan and General Marbot. Denunciations against speculators and against Schérer, the Minister of War, became frequent. Bonaparte's brothers, Joseph and Lucien, were now deputies, and the latter distinguished himself by his violent, demagogic opposition. At the very moment when the Directory's authority seemed undisputed, its fall was beginning to be prepared.

Abroad, its dictatorship cut an even poorer figure. Having quarreled inside France with the Jacobins, it started fighting their friends in the sister republics, chiefly those in Italy, and showed considerable suspicion of the generals and the contractors who protected them. The Batavian Republic was the first to feel the effects of the twenty-second of Floréal. The unitarian democrats, who in any case were at loggerheads with Daëndels and Joubert, were denounced by the Conservative notables as dangerous anarchists; Delacroix was recalled; on 24 Prairial (June 22), the government was purged and new elections assured it of a majority. In Switzerland, Rapinat saw his *coup d'état* annulled and received orders to return to France; not having been replaced, however, he remained in office, and it was he who signed the treaty of alliance. Contrary to the reputation given him by the Directory's adversaries and France's enemies, he was an honest man who did his best to make the occupation bearable, and in fact it cost the Swiss much less than the Romans, although they complained much more. The counterrevolution was still alive: the Catholic cantons rose yet again in revolt, and in October the oligarchs let the Austrians into the canton of Grisons.

The events in the Cisalpine Republic were even more distressing. The Directory sent into that region several financial agents who were hostile to the Jacobins, unpopular with the generals whom they had been sent to watch, usually capable, but chosen among the former aristocracy and thus inevitably denounced in Paris and in Italy as counter-revolutionaries: Faipoult de Maisoncelle, a former minister; Amelot de Chaillou, the son of a former minister of Louis XV, a sometime administrator of Burgundy, and a director of the emergency fund under the Constituent Assembly; Laumond, who had succeeded him in this last post after serving in the Assay Office; and Eymar, the brother of an Abbé who had figured among the "blacks" in the Constituent Assembly. Trouvé was sent with them as an ambassador; he was a tool of La Revellière, and an ambitious mediocrity. Under the influence of some Lombard nobles, the Directory declared Bonaparte's constitution null and void, and instructed Trouvé to draw up another, which, in spite of Brune, was imposed on the Cisalpine Republic. But soon the general received compensation; orders were given for this constitution to be submitted to a plebiscite, probably on the intervention of Barras, and, as Trouvé and Faipoult protested, they were replaced by Fouché and Amelot. With the connivance of the former, Brune carried out a fresh *coup* in the night of 17-18 *October*, which expelled

Trouvé's creatures from their posts; popular ratification followed. Meanwhile, Ginguené went on agitating in Piedmont, and Brune's second in command organized a demonstration in Turin, which he probably hoped would lead to disturbances that would allow his chief to occupy the country. This time the Directory got angry; Ginguené was dismissed, Fouché recalled, and Brune sent to Holland.

It was just when hostilities were beginning, the Neapolitans having invaded the Roman Republic, that the Directory took the measure which best illustrates the policy it had followed since Floréal with so little success: on 5 Frimaire, Year VII (November 26, 1798), it re-established the commissioners to the armies; three were appointed— Rapinat in Switzerland, Amelot in Milan, Faipoult in Rome. But they received no more authority than their predecessors, and their fate was even more pitiable. Joubert, who had succeeded Brune, quickly found Amelot's supervision intolerable, and tendered his resignation; the Directory finally accepted it in January, but, remaining faithful to its policy of delay, it replaced Amelot by Laumond. Schérer, who took over command of the Army of Italy, was deferential to the government's representative, and it was partly this which drew upon him the hatred of his subordinates: he would pay dear for it in the future. As soon as he arrived in Switzerland, Masséna took no notice of the civil commissioner, who asked for his recall. But it was the army that had been given the task of repelling the Neapolitans which suffered most of all. It had been entrusted to Championnet, whose conflict with Faipoult culminated in a tremendous quarrel.

The Directory had thus to a certain extent checked the activity of the propagandists, and had prevented them from revolutionizing Piedmont; but, to turn Austria away from the Coalition, it would have been necessary to go back on previous policy and there was no question of that. After the twenty-second of Floréal, François de Neufchâteau had been sent to Seltz, in Alsace, to confer with Cobenzl; he was given orders to confine himself to the Vienna incident and to refer the question of compensation to Rastatt. There, Austria could only have asked for German territory, when it was on Italy that she had designs; for the Directory, the latter country obviously remained a private preserve.

Accordingly, it carried out no real changes in its foreign policy; the fear of premature hostilities had inspired it with a certain moderation, but hesitation is not repentance. The measures taken against the Jacobins in the sister republics were simply an internal political maneuver, the logical consequence of the twenty-second of Floréal; and the supervision that the Directory tried to impose on the generals can be seen as a necessary complement of its dictatorship. Without postponing war to any significant degree, the anti-Jacobin reaction added noticeably to the general confusion, compromised the Republic's prestige, and earned for the Directory new and formidable enemies.

CHAPTER ELEVEN

Finance and
the National Economy

In spite of certain reserves, it was during the twenty months following the eighteenth of Fructidor that the Directory enjoyed its greatest authority and was least obsessed by matters of urgency. These circumstances benefited to some extent its positive achievement, which, in so many respects, prepared the way for that of the Consulate.

Financial recovery was the first task that faced it, and, as early as the evening of 19 Fructidor, the Directory had outlined its plan for this recovery in a special message. It reduced expenditure from a billion francs to six hundred million, no doubt largely thanks to peace, but also by means of that "liquidation" of the National Debt which had been considered in the spring. The Councils adopted the measure fairly quickly. This was the famous "Ramel liquidation" or "bankruptcy of the two-thirds" consecrated by the law of 9 Vendémiaire, Year VI (September 30, 1797) for the Registered Debt, and by the law of 24 Frimaire (December 14) for annuities, pensions and the Floating Debt. One-third of it was consolidated by inscription in the Great Book, or National Debt Register; the bonds could be used for the payment of taxes and for that part of the purchase price of national property payable in currency. The other two-thirds were reimbursed in bonds which could be used to pay the rest of this price, in competition with other "dead securities." The interest of the consolidated third exceeded eighty million francs, so that the budget was lightened by twice that sum, quite apart from the fact that it was relieved in arrears.

A fiscal effort was necessary nonetheless. A few measures were taken to accelerate the collection of direct taxes. A Tax Agency was set up in each department: assessment was made the responsibility of the commissioners, with the help of assessors representing the taxpayers; the drawing up of registers was entrusted to the offices of the central commissioner, who had an inspector to help him. The commissioners had a great many other responsibilities, and they lacked the necessary technical knowledge; this unsatisfactory arrangement did not produce the results which had been hoped for. The ruthless use of bailiffs was much more effective. But direct taxation, which in any case had been slightly reduced, could not be sufficient by itself. The stamp duty was extended to newspapers and posters; the monopoly of the coaching office having been abolished, a tax was imposed on the price of seats in stagecoaches; and the tolls payable on the highways were finally regularized. But the Councils went on approving expenditure without an over-all plan, and passing finance laws so late in the year that they benefited future budgets most of all; they left the new postal tariff and the increase in registration duties in abeyance. They were still extremely reluctant to approve taxes on consumption; it took them a year just to approve a slight increase in the tax on imported tobacco. The deficit for Year VI was estimated at 250 million francs. As for the burden of extraordinary expenditure, it was thrown onto the national property, which could not support it; the chief sources of income were a loan of eighty million francs for the war against England, credits obtained from the Hanseatic ports, and the exploitation of the sister republics: the Berne treasury partly financed the Egyptian expedition. Altogether, the Directory was obliged to admit that the Councils, whatever the political color of the majority, all suffered from the same defects where finance was involved.

During the summer it insisted that the budget for Year VII be approved before 1 Vendémiaire. Its wish was not granted, but at least certain laws were adopted during the autumn which for a long time were, and in some cases still are, fundamental; the patents tax of 1 Brumaire, Year VII (October 22, 1798); the stamp duty of 13 Brumaire (November 3); the land tax of 3 Frimaire (November 23); the registration duty of 22 Frimaire (December 12). The *mobilière* was reorganized on 3 Nivôse (December 23) for the third time since the Revolution; it would be reorganized yet again under the Consulate. What is more, on 4 Frimaire (November 24), the Councils decided to create a new direct tax, the tax on doors and windows, which was fixed at a modest rate and, for that reason, was paid more regularly than the rest. The situation nonetheless remained serious. In Pluviôse, after a stormy debate during which Lucien Bonaparte violently attacked the "ungodly doctrine" of the oppressors of the poor, the Five Hundred finally agreed to tax the salt from the salt marshes at the rate of one sou for each pound produced, the salt mines in the east having been leased with authority to sell theirs at two sous a pound; but the Ancients rejected the resolution. Indirect taxation had been approved only in the form of the *octroi* or town dues; it was adopted for the hospitals of Paris on 27 Vendémiaire, Year VII (October 18, 1798). In Floréal, when Ramel estimated the deficit for Year VII at sixty-six million francs, the Councils confined themselves to doubling the tax on doors and windows. Naturally, the imminent war had resulted in some attention being given to extraordinary revenue. On 26 Vendémiaire, it had been decided to sell a fresh portion of national property up to a value of 125 million francs in metallic currency, and in Ventôse holders of estates mortgaged by the Monarchy were authorized to buy the property. But the disappointments of old were repeated.

The poverty of the Treasury therefore continued; contractors and financiers retained the whip hand, and the fame grew of Ouvrard and Hinguerlot, of Paulée and Vanlerbergh, of Seguin and Madame Lange's husband Simons; the Bodin Company and many others made themselves a reputation after the Flachat and Dijon Companies. The Directory went on paying in the same coin and submitting to the same demands: it had to agree to assignments which were often advances; the "Regent" was once again put in pawn; the Batavian *rescriptions* were pledged by the million. The corruption of the financial and military agents continued. The Directory occasionally balked: in August, 1798, several of the auxiliaries of Schérer, the Minister of War, were dismissed, including his own brother; during Year VII, there were a great many agreements which granted contractors fresh assignments only in return for fresh advances, as would be the practice under the Consulate. But it is significant that the Directory was unable to impose its will on the Treasury. When it demanded from the disbursing officials a statement of account every ten days, and decided that it would authorize expenditure only to the amount of recorded funds, in order to put a stop to malpractices, the Treasury resisted to the extent of suspending all payments, and the government finally gave in. Treason even entered into it: in Thermidor, Year VI, the Treasury, in spite of the Directory's orders, paid no money to the generals entrusted with the second Irish expedition, and thus helped to bring about its failure; one of its agents, the mysterious Vannelet, boasts of the fact in one of his letters to d'Antraigues, for whom he acted as a spy.

A good many scandals revealed the seriousness of the situation. For example, the Rochefort Company, entrusted with the task of supplying the Army of the Danube, had abandoned the task but had nonetheless retained thirty-two million francs assigned to it; the Chevalier Company was paid several million francs in national property to build ships, but did not lay down a single one; while Schérer placed a huge contract for cloth with Haegmann, a small businessman in Lille who was a figurehead for Seguin, and allowed him to obtain payment by drawing on the military warehouses, which were thoroughly plundered.

The fact remains that justice has not been done to the Directory's achievement. By assuming responsibility for the bankruptcies that were an inevitable consequence of the return to metallic currency, it smoothed the way for the Consulate, which, moreover—and this is a point that historians fail to mention—completed the liquidation of the past by means of another bankruptcy. It was the laws of Year VII which laid the foundations of the country's financial reorganization. When the Directory was unable to attain its object, it did at least indicate the necessary solution, for example the creation of an autonomous administration for direct taxation, the return to moderate indirect taxation, and the subordination of the Treasury to the Executive. Even the repeated admonitions that it addressed to the Councils helped to convince public opinion that a revision of the Constitution, giving the government the right to take the initiative, was one of the necessary conditions of financial recovery. What is more, to maintain that Napoleon managed to do without the contractors and succeeded in inculcating honesty into the whole of the administration is sheer nonsense. And, of course, the Directory's contemporaries cared even less than posterity about its difficulties; in Year VII as in Year V, the Councils, irritated by its justified reproaches, used it as a scapegoat and, this time, took their revenge by overthrowing it.

The same critics who praise the Thermidorians for having suddenly returned to metallic currency and for having abruptly abandoned a planned economy make no allowance for the invincible difficulties which deflation produced for the Directorials—who, after all, were the same men— by bringing about the ruin of credit and a collapse in prices. Metallic currency reappeared only very slowly. As far as

possible, people hoarded it or bought land; the small
amount of silver and copper that the Directory managed to
mint disappeared rapidly; in Year IX, despite the victories
of the Consulate, less than a billion francs in metallic currency was in circulation, as compared with two or three
billion in 1789. Credit was accordingly rare and dear; it was
impossible to obtain a loan, with security, at less than ten
per cent, and the interest on a short-term loan was as much
as seven per cent per month. In these circumstances, how
could the Directory keep the Treasury in funds without
exorbitant sacrifices, and revive the spirit of enterprise in
order to enable the economy to bear the burden of taxation? True, a few businessmen had founded issuing banks.
In 1796, some financiers, including Perregaux and Récamier, in association with some leading merchants, founded
the Current Accounts Bank; it discounted only bills with
three signatures—in other words, it used its bank notes to
recover from its shareholders the commercial bills which
they had discounted themselves; it was a super-bank. In
order to break its monopoly, the Trade Discount Bank,
which required only two signatures, was founded on 4
Frimaire, Year VI (November 24, 1797): this was a sort
of friendly society which experienced some difficulty in
establishing itself. Other issuing banks were founded, even
in the provinces—at Rouen, for example. But, to give their
banknotes wide circulation, the Republic would have had
to accept them itself and thus turn them into a currency.
The Directory asked for nothing better. In Year VII as
before, the Councils invariably refused their consent.

To dear credit, deflation naturally adds a fall in prices.
But it is impossible to estimate its influence here, because
from 1796 to 1798 there were bumper harvests which

helped to produce the same result. In 1798, wine was also so abundant that there was a slump; on the other hand, the drought caused a crisis in breeding, but the effect on prices was the same, because the peasants had to sell their cattle cheap. In Paris, it was calculated that corn had to sell at between twenty-two and twenty-six livres a *setier* for the farmer to cover his costs: in Year VI, it sold at between eighteen and twenty livres. Generally speaking, farm prices, from Year V to Year VII, were between a quarter and a third lower than those of 1790, which had been a year of plenty; and at certain moments the fall exceeded fifty to sixty per cent in certain markets. This fall in prices naturally had some advantages for the government: it had the troops to feed, and the police reported that the common people were delighted at having finally obtained the "three eights" that they wanted most of all: bread at eight sous (for four pounds), meat at eight sous (per pound), and wine at eight sous (per pint). But it is easy to imagine how unpopular this prolonged fall in prices made the Directory with the big farmers, the well-to-do husbandmen, and the landed proprietors, from whom most of the electors were recruited. And, to return to the question of finance, it must be admitted that in these circumstances it was no mean achievement to effect a considerable reduction in tax arrears, especially when it is remembered that, under the *ancien régime*, taxation was never less than eighteen months or two years behindhand. In the Puy-de-Dôme, at the beginning of Year VII, half the land tax for Year VI had been paid, and, on the eighteenth of Brumaire, arrears had been almost completely paid up to Year V; to achieve this result, severe measures had been necessary, which again did nothing to increase the Directory's popularity.

Nor was that all. As had always happened in the old economy, the agricultural crisis reacted on industry, for, since the greater part of the population remained rural, low farm prices reduced its purchasing power. Now the manufacturers were already finding it extremely difficult to make good the losses which fixed prices, requisitioning and civil war had caused them, while the lack of credit and the continued fall in prices discouraged the spirit of enterprise. Transport, too, was meeting all sorts of difficulties. The meager yield of the toll did not make it possible to repair the roads which had been neglected since 1792, and brigandage made them anything but safe. The country's canals were few in number and maintenance work on them had come to an end. Yet inland transport should have increased since the naval war had shut down the coasting trade.

However, external trade was even more seriously affected. In 1797, only 200 seagoing vessels were left, or a tenth of the number sailing in 1789. For a long time, the neutrals had enabled French exporters to beat the English blockade; but, in return, they imported English merchandise, and in Year VI, the Directory, determined to exclude the latter, adopted a policy toward the neutrals which led them to shun French ports. The "Islands," especially Santo Domingo, which occupied such an important position in French trade at the end of the *ancien régime*, now had scarcely any contact with the mother country. The Egyptian expedition, involving as it did a break with Turkey, closed the Middle East. The Continental war had already delivered the Swiss and German markets into English hands. In Year VIII, although France had grown much bigger, her exports amounted to only 272 million francs, as compared with almost twice as much in 1789. Close union with her vassal states and allies might have helped, and the treaty with the Cisalpine Republic seemed to have been concluded with this end in view; moreover, the Councils appeared to favor a liberal customs policy: the tariff for Year IV was lower than that for 1791. But the Directory's offices, though hostile to controls at home, remained imbued with mercantilism with respect to foreign countries, and the manufacturers—who were all, especially the cotton-spinners, protectionists—laid siege to the government; indeed, they showed great bitterness about the competition of annexed Belgium. The Directory therefore tended rather to regard the sister republics as colonies to be exploited, and in this respect as in so many others, it foreshadowed the policy of the Napoleonic regime. The customs barriers with Spain, France's ally, were also strengthened at the same time.

Finally, political circumstances increased the number of crises. The eighteenth of Fructidor alarmed the rich and reduced Parisian trade; the law of 10 Brumaire, Year V, against British merchandise encouraged speculation on a rise in the price of colonial produce, and the result was a slump in Messidor, Year VI; as of the following autumn, the prospect of another Continental war had a depressing effect on business and the situation became steadily worse.

These circumstances did not augur well for the efforts which the Directory made to help producers, and for which the chief credit must go to François de Neufchâteau. Becoming Minister of the Interior again in Prairial, Year VI, he showed in fact great zeal in all the spheres he controlled: he tried to put local finance in order, drew up a plan for inland navigation, revived the statistical operations of the

Committee for Public Safety, and took an interest in public assistance and education. If it had been left to him, agriculture would have been revived, as in England, by a policy of re-allocation, and by the abolition and division of common land; he was obliged to confine himself, like the Committee of Public Safety, to issuing instructional and stimulating circulars, and to promising encouragement. He likewise appealed to the manufacturers, whom he put on their mettle by opening, on 24 Vendémiaire, Year VII (October 15, 1798), the first national exhibition, and by announcing a competition intended to reward innovators and inventors.

In point of fact, industrial production, although it was picking up again, remained lower than it had been in 1789. Lyons had twelve thousand looms before the Revolution and only 6,500 in Year XI; Carcassonne's production had fallen from sixty thousand rolls of cloth to seventeen or eighteen thousand. Technical progress remained extremely slow, and the interruption of relations with England, which provided the new machines and the workers who demonstrated them, could only harm it. As was only to be expected, it was most apparent in the cotton industry: the "jenny" came into general use, but the "mule" remained a rarity; apart from the extension of the flying shuttle, weaving was not affected; for colored materials at least, Oberkampf put the first printing machine into service in 1797. The woolen industry and metallurgy introduced no innovations. The manufacture of chemical products increased under the influence of the laboratory, but it did not use machines. The steam engine not being in use as yet, industry remained scattered, and as before, concentration occurred only in a commercial form. Great industrialists made their appearance under the Directory—Bauwens, Richard and Lenoir, Ternaux, Boyer-Fonfrède—as well as men like the Périers, Oberkampf and Chaptal, but most of them derived their power less from their factories than from work at home. Nor were their activities narrowly specialized, for as well as manufacturing, they engaged in brokerage, transport and banking.

France was still an essentially rural country. But as such, the Revolution, in proclaiming freedom of farming, had not changed the country's habits; indeed, by increasing the number of small landowners without either capital or knowledge, it had rather tended to strengthen routine. The abolition of the tithe and of seignorial rights greatly benefited the landowner, but he used the money saved to raise his standard of living or to extend his estate rather than to improve his equipment and methods. As there was no reallocation of land (on the contrary, it was parceled out to an increasing extent), enclosure remained difficult and communal practices diminished only very slightly; but the cultivation of potatoes, oleaginous plants, chicory, tobacco, and fodder plants slowly extended—a development that gave promise of a gradual reduction of fallow land. However, it was vine-growing which, since the abolition of subsidies, had made the greatest progress. Most peasants went on producing for their own needs; the speculative spirit was foreign to them as yet.

Experience had shown that France, having undertaken a national war for the first time in the history of the Great Powers, was incapable of waging it without forcing her inhabitants to reduce a standard of living which was already very low. She was accordingly faced with a choice between making peace or carrying the war abroad. The Directory was able to maintain itself in power as long as its armies lived beyond the frontiers. By bringing them back to France, defeat was to impose on the country a burden which would make it find its government intolerable. This was also the fate which lay in store for Napoleon.

CHAPTER TWELVE

Society and
the Current of Ideas

The social structure, at the time of the Directory, still bore profound traces of the revolutionary cataclysm. In Paris, the high Church, the court nobility, the farmers general, and the law and finance officers had disappeared. A breach had been made in the bourgeoisie of the *ancien régime*; the lawyers, no longer forming a corporate body and no longer buying their offices, had diminished in both numbers and prestige; and inflation, that insidious complement of revolution, had ruined the rentiers and sorely tried the property owners. The appearance of the city bore witness to the general impoverishment: the aristocratic mansions, turned into public buildings or leased to speculators who obtained money from them as best they could; the streets obstructed with impunity by the artisans and shopkeepers, and appallingly dirty; the houses allowed to go to rack and ruin, the householders no longer even having the latrines emptied, a circumstance which, in the center of Paris, exposed passers-by to the risk of unspeakable aspersions. It was the financiers and the businessmen—the Perregaux and the Récamiers, the Périers and the Chaptals—who had done best for themselves. Their ranks had been swollen by *nouveaux riches* who had made their money in speculation; but some of these, real captains of industry, rejuvenated the strength and vigor of the bourgeoisie. On a lower level, the employees paid by the State were more numerous; the writers and actors had raised themselves in public opinion; the merchants and artisans had frequently seen their affairs prosper and had become members of the middle class. The whole remained an incongruous medley and a fresh classification had still to be carried out. Next to the salons of Madame de Staël and Madame Récamier in Paris and of Madame de Condorcet at Auteuil, which remained fairly exclusive, people of very different origins and cultures could be seen rubbing shoulders in the entourage of Barras or Ouvrard and in the society of the women of easy virtue who were attached to them: Madame Tallien and Madame Fortunée Hamelin, whose scanty attire and shameless behavior have been used by anecdotal historians to characterize the France of the Directory. In Madame Angot we may see a caricature of the *nouveaux riches* who displayed their vulgar luxury and coarse arrogance in this indulgent environment.

The provinces had not been spared. The privileged social groups of which the Provincial States, the Parlements and the Clergy formed the nuclei, had broken up. In the big cities in the south of France, the Federalist crisis had made great gaps in the upper middle class. However, very much more had been preserved. A great many nobles, such as the Marquis de Ferrières, had survived and kept their lands. Here, the rentiers were less important than the landed properietors, whose capital remained and had even increased as a result of the purchase of national property; the *nouveaux riches* were less numerous and less scandalous. It was in the departments that it was most obvious that the French people had not taken Barras and Madame Tallien as their models, but on the contrary had retained their traditional habits of stubborn thrift, of a parsimonious and oppressive family life into which individualism had scarcely penetrated, and feminism even less.

This was just as true, for obvious reasons, of the country districts. The benefits of the Revolution had gone above all to those whom one might call the peasant bourgeoisie, the big farmers and the well-to-do husbandmen. However, the number of small-holders had increased, especially in those regions where the collective purchase of national property and the division of common land had favored the humble. As a result of the breaking up of big farms, farming on a modest scale had also increased. Relieved of the tithe and of seignorial rights, the peasant landowners had become as conservative as the bourgeoisie. But it would be a mistake to exaggerate the progress of this *embourgeoisement* of the nation, which in any case is a permanent feature of the history of France. The urban proletariat remained as it was; the majority of peasants still had not enough land to live on without additional earnings; and while there were somewhat fewer agricultural laborers, they remained at the mercy of unemployment and bad harvests. All that can be said is that in the midst of general deflation the workers were successful in defending their wages, which remained one-quarter or one-third higher than those of 1790: moreover the trade guilds had reappeared everywhere. The good harvests of the Directorial years therefore afforded the lower classes a temporary respite.

This society, still in the melting-pot as it were, could claim to be conforming to the aims of the Revolution, which, by proclaiming civil equality and suppressing "corporations" of all sorts, had left no other principle of social hierarchy in existence save the power of money, with its constant fluctuations. The classes that the inequality of wealth distinguished were more clearly opposed now that the social orders had disappeared. Babeuf's enterprise and the terror which it caused the bourgeoisie are sufficient proof of this, but there were concrete signs such as dress: while wig and knee-breeches had gone out of fashion, the workers wore jacket and cap, smock and bonnet, clogs rather than shoes; from one social class to the next, the "cascade of contempt" which Cournot mentions was still flowing as steadily as before 1789.

The Constitution of Year III gave the "notables" enough authority already for the reaction to continue which had been initiated after the ninth of Thermidor, against the democracy of Year II and even against certain aspects of the work of the Constituent Assembly. The promised codification was once again postponed. In the meantime, family courts and compulsory arbitration were abolished; imprisonment for debt was re-established; and divorce and the rights granted to natural children were attacked. The sale of national property, as regulated by the law of 28

Ventôse, Year IV, transferred the greater part to the bourgeoisie, and later on the restoration of auctions enabled it to benefit from the rest. In Year IV, likewise, the division of common land had been suspended, because the farmers wanted to keep it for their flocks or to lease it cheap. Under the pretext of obtaining payments of the ground rents, of which the State possessed a great number due to the clergy and the émigrés, an attempt was even made to call in question the law of July 17, 1793, which declared them null and void when one of the articles of the contract was of a feudal nature. While this attempt was abandoned, the Directory did at least reimpose on the peasants in Brittany who held annullable estates the obligation of re-purchase of which the Convention had relieved them, and it is significant that this new law on legal tenure should have been voted in the Five Hundred before the eighteenth of Fructidor and adopted by the Ancients soon afterwards, on 9 Brumaire, Year VI (October 30, 1797).

However, the reaction did not go very far, because the notables were divided. They were divided first of all by regicide and the democratic tradition of Year II; but perhaps even more by the aggressive anticlericalism which brought most of the Directorials close to the *sans-culottes*. Not that the notables who were hostile to them were all believers, but those who remained Voltairians considered —just like Voltaire, as it happens, and on account of the circumstances, with a hitherto unknown sense of urgency —that the common people had to have a religion and that the clergy was indispensable to social order; they also believed that the civil war would never really be brought to an end until peace had been made with the clergy. The Directory, on the other hand, especially after the eighteenth of

Fructidor, pursued a policy of hostility. Admittedly those priests who were neither non-juring nor deportees, who had taken the oath of hatred for the Monarchy and who abstained from all political activity, could practice their religion, but under the threat of deportation on the slightest pretext and on condition that they refrained from any external manifestation. They were not even allowed to keep registers of Catholicity or to publish banns, while their right to refuse to marry divorcees or to bury non-Catholics was sometimes disputed; they were permitted nothing which might appear to be a repudiation of civil law.

Some Directorials, moreover, like the "tyrant Robespierre," considered that the Republic could not live without a metaphysical doctrine, and would have liked to set up a civil religion in competition with Christianity. Such were La Revellière and his friend Leclerc. The majority would have nothing of it, but an attempt was made by certain private individuals. In January, 1797, the bookseller Chemin, together with a few friends, inaugurated Theophilanthropy, a moralizing, idealistic deism which brought together, in the churches of Paris, a fair number of Republicans of all shades of opinion. La Revellière acted as their patron, but his colleagues regarded the new "pope" with pitying contempt, and indeed soon began to suspect the Theophilanthropists of left-wing tendencies. With the novelty wearing off, this religion was on the decline in Year VII; moreover, it had never reached the common people. Freemasonry, whose philosophical principles were very similar, was likewise unable to do so, but in its secret gatherings it had brought together part of the bourgeoisie in a more firmly established group. In 1796, Roëttiers de Montaleau had revived the Order of the Grand Orient, and three years later, concluded an agreement with the so-called Scottish masonry; about a hundred lodges were then opened. Free-masonry thus prepared itself for the important part it was to play under the Napoleonic regime, but it remained under suspicion of Royalism at the time of the Directory, for Roëttiers had been one of Lafayette's supporters.

If most of the Directorials refused to repeat the experiment of the Religion of the Supreme Being, they were all in agreement to impose the Republican calendar—which in 1798 had become the Almanach of the Republic—and to give at long last a regular organization to the decadal and national feasts which the Convention had adopted in principle and occasionally celebrated. After the eighteenth of Fructidor, a circular from the Minister of the Interior called upon the clergy to sanctify the *décadi*, and despite Grégoire's protests, a decree of the Directory, dated 14 Germinal, Year VI (April 3, 1798), ordered all authorities to date all official acts by the Republican calendar. The laws of 17 Thermidor, Year VI (August 4) and 23 Fructidor (September 9) instituted the cessation of work on the *décadi*, though without imposing it in the individual's home, and established a list of feast days, a measure which provoked fresh conflicts with the clergy, since even the constitutional priests often refused to transfer High Mass to the *décadi*.

The Directory's policy irritated the believers by the pulling down of crosses, the banning of processions and pilgrimages, and the sale of churches where Mass was not regularly celebrated; it pushed into the arms of the extremists priests who would otherwise have tended to accept the laws; and the Republican calendar, by disturbing everybody's habits, alienated the indifferent. Altogether, without being as violent as the terrorists, the Directorials made themselves no less unbearable.

In this way, they compromised the process of de-Christianization, which in fact was continuing of its own accord. True, the faithful asserted their belief, and the hard times brought back the lukewarm Christians who, as always happens in such cases, sought moral support or consolation in the Church; but in the midst of the common people itself there was now a minority violently hostile to the clergy, and the latter was in such a deplorable condition that the future seemed bleak. Deprived of funds, and partly reduced to clandestine, itinerant worship, it obtained hardly any recruits; already inadequate in numbers, it included many aged priests who would not have successors. The practice of the sacraments therefore became more intermittent; instruction of children was often impossible; the habits of religion faded away. What is more, the clergy suffered from its divisions. The Constitutional Church, abandoned by the Republic, remained in existence, although weakened by abdications, marriages, and recantations. It still had forty-four bishops, of whome Grégoire was the most distinguished, and in 1797 they held a national council. It numbered even more priests than we are normally led to believe; in the Sarthe, a Chouan region, at least 122 have been counted, in comparison with about 200 Papists. They still had their supporters: at Sedan, three-quarters of the population remained attached to them. Moreover, it should not be forgotten that for many people the main thing was that religious worship continue; whatever their individual preference might be, they resigned themselves to accepting the constitutional priest, for want of any other. That is why the policy of de-Christianization of Year II had been a political error, and also why the Directory would have done better to deal considerately with the priests who had linked their cause with that of the Revolution. The Roman clergy fought them bitterly, but it too was divided. The non-juring priests, whose paper was the Abbé de Boulogne's *Annales ecclésiastiques*, usually condemned the *soumissionnaires*, the most famous of whom was the Sulpician Emery, and who also had their paper, the Abbé Sicard's *Annales religieuses*. They particularly attacked the *haineux* or "haters," those who had agreed to take the oath of hatred for the Monarchy. In the Sarthe, half the Roman priests took it; it is true that half the *haineux* later retracted, but the situation did not become any clearer as a result. It should be added that, separated from its bishops, most of whom had remained abroad where some lived on English subsidies, this clergy contracted independent habits and often subordinated the Church's interests to its Royalist enthusiasm. In short, the Catholic clergy was disintegrating at the same time as it was diminishing. If it had pursued a policy of secular indifference, the Directory could have counted on time to do the rest.

From its own point of view, all its efforts ought to have been directed toward education and not toward changing the calendar. The law of 3 Brumaire, Year IV, allowed freedom of education, but at the same time confirmed the establishment of secular public schools, a measure which rendered the reconstitution of a *de facto* Church monopoly impossible. In this respect, the primary school was of capital importance. Possibly the Directory would have recognized this if it had not been short of money and personnel; however, more than one Thermidorian considered, as did Voltaire, that the common people had no time for education and that, moreover, it would be of no use to them. An opinion of this sort was even more common with regard to women, whatever their station in life. In any case, the law of 3 Brumaire chiefly concerned the higher and secondary levels intended to prepare the sons of the bourgeoisie for the liberal professions, and the Directory enforced it with this end in view. Since the great establishments of higher education, chiefly devoted to the sciences, had been founded or reorganized by the Convention, all the Directory had to do was to install the Institut which was to undertake the control of research. There remained the task of opening the "central schools"; each department was to have its own, and they did in fact have them, with very few exceptions. The local administration maintained them and appointed the masters on the advice of a jury, so that this secondary education was largely decentralized, whereas higher education, with the exception of two medical schools, had been concentrated in Paris. At the central school, the classes, divided into three successive series, each of two years, were optional; the sciences occupied a considerable place in them and were preferred. But the French language, which was not taught in all the colleges under the *ancien régime*, also occupied a place of honor; if the ancient languages were not eliminated, still they had ceased to be the basis of the educational system, and sometimes the modern languages were admitted on an equal footing. Several of these schools had remarkable masters, and some of them, those in the Doubs for example, were very successful. However, they were reproached for not providing elementary tuition, for not forming study courses, and for not maintaining supervision and discipline, so that they resembled institutes of higher education rather than colleges for adolescents. What is more, they had no boarding facilities. It was suggested that the Councils should found preparatory "secondary schools" and a "national Prytaneum" at which the Republic would maintain 1,200 scholarship students. But, in this respect again, the foundations were laid for the Consulate's achievement and nothing more. As for the primary schools, each department established a certain number, but not one in each commune; the central administration also appointed the teachers, who were selected by a jury; it likewise appointed women teachers, whereas there were no secondary schools for girls. The municipal administration had to provide premises for the school and accommodation for the teacher; but it was not obliged to pay the latter, whose school fees might be his only source of income. Recruiting was totally inadequate in both quantity and quality; and it remained inadequate, for there were no training colleges for teachers. In Year VII the Five Hundred were asked to re-establish payment of the primary-school teacher by the Republic, but in vain. Where would the Republic have found the money? Moreover, experience showed that parents were far from eager to send their children to school, except to prepare them for their first communion. The secular character of public education therefore hindered its progress, and it goes without saying that, for the Directory, there could be no question of abandoning it. Consequently there were private primary and secondary schools everywhere, which more often than not were denominational. The Directory placed them under the supervision of the municipal authorities, forbade civil servants to send their children to them, and decided to choose its agents only from the pupils of the public schools. It does not appear that these last two measures had the slightest effect, but inspection and obligatory attendance at decadal ceremonies led to the compulsory or voluntary closing of several private schools.

The experiment, having lasted barely two years, did not enable the Directory to exert a positive influence on the education of the young people of France. In any case, circumstances would not have favored it. Brought up more or less haphazardly during these troubled times, and embittered by the memory of the hardships that had darkened their early years, the growing generations were even more inclined than usual to run counter to their parents and thought of nothing but enjoying themselves. Those who were ambitious tended to turn towards the army, in which they could make a career for themselves, if they were courageous, without needing to have learned anything. One and all rejected idealism; contemporaries are agreed in recording their unscrupulous utilitarianism. The Revolution could not find cause for self-congratulation in this, but neither could the counterrevolution, for these young men had no desire to return to the *ancien régime*. It was a time when the life of the spirit was not held in particularly high honor, and indeed it had nothing original to offer.

Rationalism was, in a sense, the official philosophy. Represented by the "Ideologues," it held full sway at the Institut. Under the influence of English thought, it had repudiated apriorism and the deductive method of the Cartesians, as well as all metaphysical preoccupations, to become experimental and positivist. Destutt de Tracy's aim was to determine, by means of observation, how ideas are formed, whence the name of the School; the doctor Cabanis was working in the direction of experimental and pathological psychology. Morality for them meant a knowledge of customs and manners. Ginguené and Fauriel introduced historical and relativistic criticism into the study of literature and the arts. The sciences, which were making steady progress, served as a rampart for rationalism, whatever the personal opinions of the scientists might be, and this is why conservatives and reactionaries have always tended to cut down the scientific share of education. In 1796, Laplace had just published his *Système du monde*; Lagrange and Monge were famous; for the time being, France had no great physicists, but chemistry could boast Berthollet and several others; Haüy was creating crystallography; Lamarck, Cuvier and Geoffroy-Saint-Hilaire were beginning to teach at the Museum; while Bichat was about to publish the results of his research into tissues.

Those who hated the Revolution rejected the rationalism of the eighteenth century, even when it remained idealistic and deistic, as being responsible for the catastrophe which had overtaken France. A return to tradition and revealed religion was advocated by the philosophical turncoats: La Harpe, who had become a Fideist, or Fontanes, who invoked social utility. A similar evolution was taking place in émigré circles, and it was outside France that Bonald and Maistre published their first works in 1796. Adapting experimental rationalism to justify tradition, after the manner of Burke, they would become the masters of the counterrevolution in the nineteenth century, but the Directory's contemporaries knew nothing of them. A work that obtained speedier success was the *Mémoires pour servir à l'histoire du jacobinisme*, which the Abbé Barruel published in 1797 to reduce the Revolution to the level of a Masonic plot.

In the world of ideas, what threatened the supremacy of

rationalism most of all was Rousseau's influence, which was greater than ever, in spite of the disfavor with which people viewed his political theories. He had set feeling against reason, and had held intuition to be the true instrument of knowledge, to such a degree that it opened up the moral world and even the supernatural by means of direct contact with God. The common reader appreciated his sensual sentimentalism most of all, but his mysticism had certain links with the vague, esoteric doctrines which had abounded in the eighteenth century and which were classed together under the name of Illuminism. France had not entirely escaped these doctrines: Saint-Martin, the "unknown philosopher," was still alive; Alsace and Lyons remained two centers of mysticism. These tendencies would inspire, in Germany, a "Romantic" philosophy which later exerted a certain influence in France, without ever having been thoroughly taught there.

In France, Romanticism remained a type of feeling, a literary and artistic form of individualism, a reaction against classical art. Under the Directory, however, nobody foresaw that the latter was going to be dethroned, and Pre-Romanticism is all that one can talk about at this time, Classical literature was still highly regarded, the classical tradition being maintained by writers who were distinguished even if devoid of genius: Ducis, Arnault, Andrieux, Delille, and "Pindar" Lebrun. But it was on the decline, for the society that had witnessed its birth had disappeared and its effects were exhausted. The *nouveaux riches* and the members of the petty bourgeoisie who had not had a college education could not appreciate its inspiration and its allusions to Greek and Latin sources; they far preferred Pixérécourt's melodramas and the novels of Pigault-Lebrun and Ducray-Duménil, which were the origins of Romantic drama. Bernardin de Saint-Pierre's work *Paul et Virginie*, which dated from 1787, was still read with undiminished enthusiasm. The "troubadour style," made fashionable by the Comte de Tressan, and popularized by songs and engravings, foreshadowed the Romantic cult of a conventional medievalism. The Romantics of other countries were also beginning to be appreciated, and there was nothing to equal the extraordinary fame obtained under the Directory by Ossian's poems, manufactured by MacPherson about thirty years before.

The return to antiquity, which had characterized the end of the *ancien régime*, did not revitalize literature: Chénier's poems had remained unpublished. But it had revived memories of their college days among the orators and journalists of the Revolution, and this constantly became apparent at the time of the Directory. It had imposed itself particularly on the painters and sculptors: it was in 1799 that David exhibited his *Sabines*. However, this revival of antiquity also benefited Alexandrine art, so-called Etruscan motifs, and even Egyptian ornaments; and thus, in decorative art at least, the eighteenth-century tradition had been maintained in a parallel fashion, while acquiring elements which foreshadowed the "Empire" style. Like the "Louis XVI" style, that of the Directory was heterogeneous.

In the spiritual sphere as in politics, it was a period of transition. Perhaps it reveals, more clearly than other periods easier to characterize, that of the different tendencies which offer themselves to the mind, none is ever effaced, even when one of them seemed to have obtained final supremacy.

CHAPTER THIRTEEN

The Egyptian Expedition and the Second Coalition

Approved on 15 Ventôse, Year VI (March 5, 1798), and prepared with the greatest secrecy, the Egyptian expedition comprised thirteen ships of the line, seventeen frigates, thirty-five other warships, 280 transport craft, 16,000 sailors, 38,000 officers and troops, and also a commission of 187 scientists, writers and artists including Berthollet, Monge and Geoffroy-Saint-Hilaire. It was nearly called off again as a result of the incident in which Bernadotte had been involved in Vienna, for Bonaparte had taken the affair in hand and offered to place himself at the head of the army if war broke out. Barras even claims that he had to order him to set off. It is possible that Barras exaggerated the part he played, but it is also possible that Egypt would have lost its attraction for Bonaparte if hostilities had opened again in Europe. Whatever the truth of the matter, he left Toulon on 30 Floréal (May 19).

Progress was slow and he did not reach Malta until June 6; the Grand Master of the Order that had been installed there since the sixteenth century had allowed himself to be bribed, and handed over the island without firing a shot. Continuing on its way, the fleet only narrowly missed Nelson. He was looking for it everywhere, went ahead of it without knowing, landed at Alexandria and set off again for the Aegean Sea, while behind him Bonaparte was disembarking. After seizing the port, the army hugged the Nile, skirmishing with the Mamelukes; then, on July 21, it routed them near the Pyramids and entered Cairo. Bonaparte then pursued Ibrahim, one of the two leaders, as far as the isthmus, while Desaix was pushing Mourad back beyond Assuan. Meanwhile, Nelson had returned to Sicily, where the complicity of the Neapolitans enabled him to rest and refit; informed at last of his adversary's whereabouts, he appeared, in the evening of July 31, in the Aboukir roads, where Brueys' squadron was lying at anchor pending orders from Bonaparte to return to Corfu. On August 1, it was destroyed and its commander killed. This terrible disaster, which imprisoned Bonaparte in his conquest with no hope of returning home or obtaining reinforcements, had tremendous repercussions throughout Europe. On September 9, Turkey declared war on France and, under the protection of the victorious admiral, the Neapolitans decided to invade the Roman Republic.

In spite of all this, Bonaparte went on organizing his

conquest as if it were to be lasting; after the Cisalpine Republic, his genius found a new testing-ground here. His policy consisted in leaving the native administration in place, but under supervision; in other words, he established a protectorate. At the same time he inaugurated an embryonic representative government by instituting a municipal divan in Cairo, another in each province, and finally a general divan, all composed of notables chosen by himself: his concept of the constitutional regime was a system of consultative bodies appointed by the government, and his social policy consisted in attaching the notables to himself by entrusting them with the administration. He also fixed his religious policy in Egypt: since the population was almost entirely Moslem, he turned Moslem, he said later; in other words he displayed a profound respect for Islam and its prophet, and heaped favors upon its leaders. The enlightened despot nonetheless undertook, with relentless energy, the modernization of the country—taking sanitary measures against the plague, putting the canals back into service, creating a postal service, opening the first printing-works, setting up the first windmills, and making plans to substitute irrigation for inundation, and to link the Nile to the Red Sea. The commission he had taken with him became the Cairo Institute, and its work prepared that famous *Description de l'Égypte* which was the most lasting result of the expedition. This policy came into conflict with the Moslems' incurable mistrust, expecially as Turkey, with the help of English propaganda, urged them to wage a holy war on the French: isolated soldiers and small outposts were attacked, and the nomads never relented. All the same, the majority of the population would probably have resigned itself if the army had not been obliged to live on the country by means of taxes, levies and confiscations. To make sure that taxes were paid and his funds increased, Bonaparte demanded the registration of landed properties and the payment of taxes on changes of ownership, legal documents, and certificates of birth, marriages and deaths. The result was a terrrible insurrection in Cairo on October 21, and a bloody repression.

Besides, it was known in Egypt that Turkey was preparing to invade the country by land and sea with the support of an English squadron. At the end of the winter, Bonaparte decided to go and destroy the army which was gathering there; he set off in February, 1799, with 15,000 men, crossed the desert, and advanced as far as Acre without meeting much resistance. But the Pasha Djezzar and the émigré Philippeaux defended the town stubbornly, and after Sidney Smith had captured the ships which were bringing the siege artillery, Bonaparte finally retreated on May 20. He returned to Egypt, not without sustaining losses on the way. He had at least delayed the Turkish attack on the isthmus, but soon afterwards an army landed at Aboukir; it was destroyed there on July 25. However, there was no way out of the situation, and it was in vain that the Directory had tried to send Bruix to help. In August, Bonaparte, leaving his army to Kléber, went off to seek adventure in France.

At this time, it was nearly a year since his initiative had set the Second Coalition on foot. After the Turks, the Russians had joined in. The Tsar and the Sultan formed an alliance, and the Russian fleet was allowed to pass through the Straits to go and attack the Ionian Isles: Corfu was the last to fall, on March 3, 1799. The Egyptian expedition had thus provided the Russians with access to the Mediterranean and a position in the Ottoman Empire which they have never recovered since. The Tsar hoped for even better things: he appointed himself the protector of the Order of Malta and of the King of the Two Sicilies. The English had lost no time in giving their support to the Russo-Turkish entente; they were blockading Malta and were in control at Naples. On December 29, an Anglo-Russian alliance finally came to the main point: it was decided that they should make combined landings in Italy and Holland and that Russian troops based in Jersey should threaten Brittany.

A month earlier, either out of conceit or out of misplaced confidence in the speed of their protectors, the Neapolitans had gone ahead, under the leadership of the Austrian Mack, and occupied Rome. They had thus provided the propagandists with a supreme success. The Directory declared war on their king, and also on the King of Sardinia, who was regarded as an accomplice and withdrew to Cagliari; the whole of Piedmont was occupied without a shot being fired. Championnet had withdrawn his little army behind the Tiber. Attacked at Civita-Castellana, he routed his adversaries, re-entered Rome, and, taking the offensive in his turn, occupied Naples on January 23, 1799. He made a show of ignoring Faipoult, the Civil Commissioner. On the way, the army and a good many of its commanders had engaged in looting, and the Castle of Caserte, the Neapolitan Versailles, had been cleaned out. In Naples, all the public coffers were seized by the generals, and Championnet made it clear that he regarded himself as the Bonaparte of southern Italy: after joining up with the Liberals, he proclaimed the "Parthenopian Republic," the government of which he entrusted to them, promising to content himself with a levy of sixty million. Faipoult intervened to enforce both his own levies and the intentions of the Directory. The latter did not want another republic; it was keeping the new conquest as exchange currency and had urged that it should be thoroughly exploited, thus returning to the policy of 1796. Faipoult insisted that all prizes of war should be handed over to him, gave orders that crown property and the goods of those émigrés who had followed the King of Sicily should be sequestrated, and imposed a monthly levy upon the country. Championnet stood up to him and finally expelled him. As usual, the Directory recalled both of them; but soon, better informed, it had the general arrested and summoned before a court martial; several of his subordinates suffered the same fate or were cashiered. For the first time, the Directory was trying to bring the generals to heel: they would help to overthrow it.

The Coalition needed the support of Austria or Prussia to launch an attack on the Adige, in Switzerland and on the Rhine. Prussia showed a certain reticence; however, when the Directory sent Sieyès to Frederick William III with yet another proposal for an alliance with the Republic, the King had him shown the door. Thugut negotiated while refusing to enter into any engagements: he knew that the Tsar wanted to restore the Italian sovereigns whose spoils he coveted, and that England wanted most of all to reconquer the Netherlands, in which he was uninterested. War broke out without his having signed anything, and from the outset the Second Coalition, like the First, carried within itself the seeds of its failures and its final disintegration. All the same, Thugut prepared for war and authorized the Russians to cross Austrian territory. The Directory made this a *casus belli* on 22 Ventôse, Year VII

(March 12, 1799). Tuscany was promptly occupied and Pius VI taken to Valence where he died in August. A bloody incident fixed the character of war in the eyes of the revolutionaries. During the night of April 28, as the French plenipotentiaries were leaving Rastatt, they were attacked by Austrian hussars. One of them, Jean Debry, escaped; the other two, Roberjot and Bonnier, were killed. It is still uncertain who was responsible for these murders; in France they were seen as a manifestation of the hatred that the kings and the aristocracy had vowed for the Republic and as proof that the counterrevolution was beginning a new crusade.

Since the autumn, the Directory had been getting ready to withstand the attack. After the eighteenth of Fructidor the reawakening of the revolutionary spirit had revived the question of the general mobilization of the nation. Debry had even put forward, though unsuccessfully, a plan for the military training of French youth. On a more modest scale, Jourdan, on 23 Nivôse, Year VI (January 12, 1798), had proposed the formation of an auxiliary army of 100,000 men chosen by ballot; since this method of selection was criticized as contrary to the principle of equality, he prepared a new project which became the law of 19 Fructidor, Year VI (September 5, 1798), known as the Jourdan Law or the Conscription Law. It inaugurated compulsory military service between the ages of twenty and twenty-five, with exemption only for men who had married before 23 Nivôse, Year VI. The conscripts fit for duty were to be registered on a national list, in five classes and according to their dates of birth. If a levy was necessary, the Legislature decided on a contingent which the Minister of War called to the colors, beginning with the youngest.

Those who refused to answer the call were deprived of civic rights and even of certain civil rights. On 28 Nivôse, Year VII (January 17, 1799), another law annulled the dispensations and exemptions granted since 1793.

Immediately after the Jourdan Law had been passed, an initial levy was decided on. The law of 3 Vendémiaire, Year VII (September 24, 1798) fixed it at 200,000 men. As before, considerable difficulties arose. The registration details were incomplete or nonexistent; no provision had been made for the medical examinations, which the Minister had to leave to boards composed of fathers whose sons were affected by the Law, a fact which gave rise to scandalous abuses; it proved impossible in practice to draw up the national list of conscripts. Their number was put at 203,000, including those who had already been invalided out; 143,000 were found fit for duty, a figure which represented a huge wastage. Only 97,000 answered the call to colors, and these were sent to join the armies in isolated detachments, a practice which facilitated desertion; only 74,000, or fifty-one per cent of the total, joined their units. On 28 Germinal, Year VII (April 17, 1799), the Legislature decided that the numbers of the prescribed contingent should be made up, but it made serious alterations to the Jourdan Law: those liable to conscription were authorized to meet beforehand to find volunteers to complete the contingent or to draw lots among themselves; what is more, the conscripts marked down for call-up were allowed to provide a replacement. Nonetheless, only 71,000 men answered the summons, 57,000 of whom reached the front.

The Directory's army had become a professional army. This flood of conscripts gave it, by means of a fresh amalgamation, something of the popular character of the army of Year II. But it was not sufficiently reinforced for the opening of the campaign, and, unlike its predecessor, it did not have the advantage of numerical superiority over the enemy. Nor was it properly supplied. It was in order to clothe, equip and arm the conscripts that the Legislature put on sale, as we have seen, 125 million francs' worth of national property, and the great fiscal laws of Year VII bear witness to an effort to pay for the war; but it was a belated, inadequate effort. The conscripts were sent to the front before they were completely ready; and as for the armies, living on vassal or enemy countries which were already exhausted, they were in a state of destitution. In Italy, their principal source of supply was recently occupied Piedmont, which was thoroughly exploited.

In the over-all concept of the campaign, the spirit of the new warfare was totally lacking. The Army of the Danube, numbering 45,000 men and under Jourdan's command, was given the task of invading southern Germany. Of the 100,-000 men who were in Italy, Schérer was able to assemble only 45,000 on the Adige. Between the two of them, Masséna was to conquer the Canton of Grisons and threaten the Tyrol. The French therefore attacked everywhere at once, on a long front, instead of using Switzerland by establishing a main striking force there which could be moved at will into Italy or Germany to obtain a decision. The Austrians were set out in the same way: the Archduke Charles had 75,000 men in Bavaria; Kray had 60,000 in Venetia; and 20,000 more guarded the Tyrol. They appear to have been unaware of their numerical superiority, and waited for the Russians before committing themselves completely. Moreover, Thugut subordinated Austrian military operations to his political schemes. The campaign, slow-moving and disjointed, displayed all the characteristics of a war of the *ancien régime*.

It was Masséna who obtained the greatest success; he occupied the Canton of Grisons, but, entering Vorarlberg, came to grief before Feldkirch. Jourdan advanced as far as Lake Constance and attacked the Archduke at Stokach on March 25; repulsed, he brought his army back to the Rhine and handed in his resignation; on this front, the Archduke was unable to press forward, for Thugut sent him to invade Switzerland. Schérer carried the fortified positions of Pastrengo and Rivoli, but his attack on Verona was badly planned and tried his army sorely; attacked in his turn at Magnano, on April 5, he beat a retreat, although the battle had been indecisive, and, without trying to resist anywhere, withdrew as far as the Adda before handing the army over to Moreau. Kray was not very forceful either: he waited for Suvoroff, who brought along 20,000 Russians and assumed supreme command. This general, famous for his victories over the Turks and the Poles, was a remarkable trainer of men rather than a strategist. Between April 25 and 27, he attacked the crossings of the Adda and forced several of them, notably at Cassano; the Sérurier division was destroyed or captured; Moreau evacuated the region of Milan and re-assembled the debris of his army at Alessandria. Suvoroff staged a triumphal entry into Milan, but then dispersed a good part of his troops and waited until May 12 before attacking Moreau, without much success. All the same, the French withdrew again as far as Coni.

Moreau was counting on Macdonald who, with exceptional slowness, was bringing the Naples troops back up the rebellious peninsula. Instead of summoning Macdonald to join him, he arranged to meet him near Alessandria.

Macdonald crossed the Apennines, only to find his way barred by Suvoroff on the banks of the Trebia. The battle lasted three days, from July 17 to 19: having failed to break through, Macdonald went back across the mountains and, hugging the coast, made his way to Genoa. Moreau, who had advanced victoriously as far as Marengo, fell back to join him.

The setbacks in Germany and Italy led to a withdrawal by Masséna; he had to evacuate the Canton of Grisons and, since the Archduke had crossed the Rhine, fall back on the Limmat. Attacked, he won the first Battle of Zürich, on June 4, but he thought fit to cross back over the river and abandon the town. He took up a position between the Rhine and Lake Zug, covered by the Limmat and Lake Zürich. But as Lecourbe had been obliged to abandon the St. Gotthard Pass and the valley of the Reuss, he was open to attack from the rear by an army coming from Italy.

Summer had come, and there was every reason to expect some large-scale operations; the Coalition forces could converge on Switzerland, crush Masséna, and enter France through the Burgundy gateway. But nothing of the sort happened, and for two months hostilities were, so to speak, suspended. Italian fortresses, even Mantua, fell to Suvoroff with an incredible rapidity which aroused suspicions of treason; having obtained control of Piedmont, his only thought was to install the King there and invade Dauphiné. Thugut was anxious to find a way of getting him to leave Italy by sending him into Switzerland, and he suggested to the Tsar that the liberation of that country was a task worthy of the savior of Europe; in fact, his only concern was the political profit to be derived from this maneuver. As in 1793, the Coalition Powers thus gave the

Republic a breathing space; however, the French armies, despite the government's exhortations, remained incapable of undertaking anything until the end of the summer, and long before then the war had provoked decisive events in France.

CHAPTER FOURTEEN

The Crisis of Year VII

At the beginning of Germinal (late March, 1799), the campaign had scarcely begun and there had been no setback to obliterate the memory of the easy conquest of Naples. However, the elections promised to be unfavorable to the Directory, for since the autumn, well before war had been declared, its oppressive influence had been felt in the stagnation of business, the growth of taxation, and above all in conscription. True, since 1793, absentees and conscripts had been pursued, but no contingent had been called up; if there had been such an ardent longing for peace, it had been largely out of fear of a fresh levy. Now it had come. The mediocre result that it yielded bears witness to its unpopularity; moreover, it was not carried out without trouble. In November, 1798, part of the Belgian countryside rose in revolt: this "war of the peasants" lasted two months and left the country highly disturbed. In France, fear of a new Vendée insurrection had been so lively that the Directory had been authorized to suspend enforcement of the law in the west; the Chouans nonetheless acquired new strength, and in March the town of Château-Gontier was taken by surprise. Everywhere, the rebel bands were swollen by absentees and deserters, and their attacks became more frequent.

Most of the public blamed the Directory for having provoked the war, while the Jacobins accused it of having failed to make the necessary preparations, and of allowing the counterrevolution once again to play the enemy's game. The Directorial majority, conscious of the electors' anxiety and discontent, threw the responsibility on the government —as always happens in such cases—but not without a certain genuine feeling, since it was irked by the Directors' dictatorship. Resorting to the traditional diversion, the Directory denounced the partnership of Royalists and Anarchists in the enemy's service. "Just as the campaign is opening," declared the *Moniteur*, "it is at home that the first blows are struck." During the elections, at least, the Royalists lay low as in Year VI and for the same reasons: it was the Jacobins who were under attack. A circular issued by François de Neufchâteau tried to revive fear of the Terror and frighten the rich:

No more brigands in office, no more scoundrels in power.
. . . Would you like to see the law of the *maximum* reim-

posed? Would you like to see Féraud's murderers reappear carrying his bleeding head on a pike?

In preparation for the elections, the usual methods were used: massive dismissals, instructions to the commissioners, the dispatch of special agents to a score of departments, and the organization of secessions; in the Doubs and the Sarthe, official pressure created a scandal. However, it was not as energetic as in Year VI, probably because the Directory or its officials were aware of a hostility they could not hope to overcome. Indeed, it was often enough for a candidate to be recommended by the government for him to be defeated: out of 187 who had been recommended more or less openly, 121 were beaten. Since the law of 12 Pluviôse, Year VI, was still in force, could not the device of the twenty-second of Floréal be repeated? The attitude adopted by the Councils ruled out this possibility: they systematically validated the choices of the original assemblies.

As the Directory had aimed its attack chiefly against the Jacobins, its defeat was regarded as their victory. Yet this was not the case. The Thermidorian bourgeoisie still formed the majority and it was not long before this became obvious. As it was violently hostile to the Directors, it came to an agreement with the Jacobins to overthrow them, but its political and social tendencies remained those of the government it had turned out. The crisis therefore took place in three stages: the fall of the Second Directory, the apparent triumph of the Left, and a violent and vigorous anti-Jacobin reaction.

During the weeks following the elections, the situation of the Republic underwent a disastrous deterioration. Italy was lost, Switzerland invaded, Holland threatened. At home, administration was disorganized by the Royalists' guerrilla warfare and by passive resistance to civic obligations. "Everything is going to pieces," stated a report of 18 Prairial. Hostility to the Directors increased as a result; they were clearly incapable of making either peace or war. Was this simple incompetency? To have tolerated the wastefulness which emptied the military depots and condemned the army to destitution was criminal negligence at the very least. The addresses which started coming in from the departments openly accused Schérer of treason. The generals joined in the chorus of blame in order to explain their defeats, avenge their disgrace, and avoid the prosecution to which they had rendered themselves liable. Their collusion with the opposition, already visible in the press and in speeches, is obvious from the place that the Five Hundred gave them in their lists of candidates in the course of the crisis: one of these lists included seven generals and admirals out of ten names. As of the end of Germinal, the examination of the financial measures that had become indispensable strained relations between the Directory and the Councils to the breaking point. Once again, the *rapporteur*, who was Génissieu, reduced the deficit to nothing and triumphantly recalled the credits that had been voted; Ramel once again pertinently refuted his arguments. In Floréal, a rumor began to spread that the Directory was preparing a *coup de force*: but this was impossible, since the Directory had quarreled with the generals, and the latter, defeated and humiliated, were incapable of imitating Bonaparte and Hoche.

In any case, even before the new Councils had met on 1 Prairial, chance had declared itself, contrary to Year V, against the Directors; on 20 Floréal, when they drew lots to discover which one was to retire, it was Reubell, the most intelligent member of the government, who was indicated by the ballot. Then, after the Five Hundred had proposed General Lefebvre, who was reputed to be a good Jacobin, in the first place, the Ancients, on 27 Floréal (May 16), rejected him in favor of Sieyès by 118 votes out of 205. Sieyès was known to be hostile to the Directors; it was also known that he was full of contempt for the Constitution of Year III, which had been preferred to his own, and that he wanted to change it. His election showed that hostilities had opened and indeed that there was a large majority of the Ancients in favor of revision. Barras had contributed to Sieyès' success—possibly because he was not opposed to the idea of revision, more probably to ensure his own survival now that the fall of the Second Directory seemed likely. The Trojan horse was in position, but probably few people imagined that Sieyès, the theoretician of the liberal representative system, was going to dig its grave.

Returning from Berlin, he was unable to take his seat in the Directory until 21 Prairial (June 9); ten days were enough for him to attain his object, a fact which makes one wonder whether this "revolutionary mole," as Robespierre called him, had not been at work for a long time. In the Five Hundred, Boulay, Bertrand du Calvados, Poullain-Grandprey, and Bergasse-Laziroule were his spokesmen; he probably manipulated the Jacobins through Lucien Bonaparte, and the generals through Joubert, the commanding officer of the seventeenth military division, whom he appears to have chosen as the instrument of his future *coup d'état*. All of a sudden, on 28 Prairial (June 16), Poullain-

Grandprey recalled that the message of the seventeenth, asking the Directory for an *exposé* of the military situation, had remained unanswered, and obtained a decision that the Five Hundred should stay in permanent session until an answer arrived; the Ancients followed their example. The Five Hundred also ordered their commissions to meet to consider what measures should be taken—an order of dubious legality—and the real discussion was thus taken outside the Assembly; then, about eleven o'clock at night, the hall filled up and Bergasse, suddenly attacking Treilhard's election, got a resolution passed which expelled him from the Directory and which the Ancients promptly ratified. The motive invoked had been implicitly rejected in Year VI, as has been seen; and besides, a month before, a deputy had been validated who was not of the legal age at the time of his election, on the ground that he would attain that age before 1 Prairial. La Revellière therefore proposed, that same night, that the Directors should not promulgate the law, but as Sieyès and Barras declared themselves in agreement with the Councils, Treilhard withdrew; on the twenty-ninth, his place was filled by Gohier, the President of the Court of Appeal, who had been Minister of Justice in Year II and was considered to be sympathetic towards the Jacobins. On the thirtieth, Bertrand returned to the attack, this time against La Revellière and Merlin, openly accusing them of misappropriation and treason; then Boulay denounced "the subjection of the Legislature" and the factious resistance which had been envisaged during the night of the twenty-eighth; several representatives called for an indictment, and Joubert and Bernadotte made threatening remarks. However, Sieyès, Barras, and the majority wanted a peaceful solution, and as it turned out the crisis was solved behind the scenes. As early as the twenty-ninth, Sieyès had asked his colleagues to resign; on the thirtieth, Barras, failing to overcome their resistance, made a terrible scene. Deputies came along to advise them to submit; finally the Ancients formed an unofficial delegation which came and begged them to give way in the interests of the Republic. Merlin, utterly terrified, capitulated first, and La Revellière resigned himself to following his example. On 1 and 2 Messidor, their places were filled by Roger-Ducos, a regicide member of the Convention, then a magistrate in the Landes, proposed by Sieyès, and by Moulin, an obscure general and good Jacobin, chosen by Barras. All the ministers were successively replaced, not excepting Talleyrand.

The *journée* of the thirtieth of Prairial, Year VII (June 18, 1799) was therefore not a *coup d'état*: the two Directors had not dared to face a perfectly legal indictment; but the event involved an interpretation of the Constitution which the Directory had never accepted and which, giving the Legislature power over the Executive, tended towards a parliamentary system. As early as 3 Messidor, François de Nantes, on behalf of a commission of eleven set up on 29 Prairial, presented a complex and confused project adopted on the ninth, of which several articles, restricting the Directory's authority, emphasize this aspect of the crisis, although the Ancients postponed and finally refused ratification. However, if the thirtieth of Prairial was a ninth of Thermidor insofar as it changed the personnel of the government to suit the Councils, it did not subordinate it or weaken it, as the Thermidorian Committees had been subordinated and weakened: the Directory retained the duration and the authority laid down by the Constitution. It is true that it had not gained in either prestige or unity; but Sieyès imposed his opinions on it, and, in his stubborn determination to bring about the downfall of the regime, he displayed a skill and a firmness that form a striking contrast with the feebleness he showed on the eighteenth of Brumaire.

Then again, the thirtieth of Prairial was the *journée* of the generals. Bernadotte was given the Ministry of War; Joubert was put in command of the Army of Italy; as for Championnet, he was released from prison, the charge against him was dropped, his subordinates were released and replaced, and he was put at the head of an Army of the Alps which was formed to bar the way to Suvoroff. The commissioners to the armies were finally stripped of all authority: Rapinat's resignation had been accepted, while Joubert, on his arrival in Italy, told Laumond that since he no longer had any conquered territory to control, there was nothing for him to do, and sent him back to France.

Finally, the thirtieth of Prairial was a revenge for the twenty-second of Floréal: the three new Directors were "Floréalists" and the appointment of Robert Lindet, some-time member of the great Committee of Public Safety, as Minister of Finance seemed symbolic. This impression was confirmed by the numerous dismissals which followed and the appointment of leading Jacobins such as Raisson, Chaudieu, or General Marbot who took Joubert's place at the head of the seventeenth division. The resolution of 9 Messidor abrogated the law of 19 Fructidor, extended in Year VI, which had suspended the freedom of the press; the Ancients decided to ratify this article on 14 Thermidor (August 1), but the newspapers had not waited to prolif-erate. It is true that most of them were hostile to the Republic, but the clubs also reopened, and they were generally dominated by the Jacobins. One report states that there were soon over forty in Paris; the most famous one met as of 18 Messidor (July 6) in the hall which the Five Hundred had left in Year VI for the former Palais Bourbon, and was therefore generally known as the Club du Manège or the Riding-School Club. The first "regulator" was Drouet, Babeuf's accomplice; 250 deputies joined the Club and there were up to 3,000 members.

That the thirtieth of Prairial was above all a victory for the Jacobins was also the impression given by the passing of the famous laws that the Left obtained immediately afterward by invoking the dangers threatening the Republic— not only because the majority was by no means insensitive to those dangers, but also because this majority, still excited by its struggle with the Directors, took a few days to realize that it was on a slippery slope leading to a new revolutionary government.

Proposed by Jourdan on 9 Messidor (June 27), the law of the tenth provided, as he said, for the *levée en masse:* all five classes of conscripts were called up in their entirety; at the same time, the system of replacements was abolished, and leaves granted since 1793 were submitted to departmental military commissions for revision. The number of men liable for conscription was estimated at 223,000, and the number of those who left for the front at 116,000. A month later, another law gave orders for the reorganization of the National Guard—a necessary measure, for flying columns could be drawn from it to fight for rebels and the brigands.

After men, it was the turn of property. Requisitioning increased again, this time openly encouraged by instructions from the Directory to the departmental authorities. Above all, the compulsory loan was reintroduced, again proposed by Jourdan on 9 Messidor, immediately adopted in principle, and fixed at 100 million francs. Considerable difficulty was experienced in fixing the conditions, which became law only on 19 Thermidor (August 6). The loan, fixed in accordance with a graduated scale, affected those who paid at least 300 francs in land tax, as well as investment incomes impartially estimated by a jury of citizens not liable to the loan, over and above 10,000 francs, though a speculative fortune could be taxed on the whole of the yield.

Then there came a repressive law, the Law of Hostages of 24 Messidor (July 12). In those departments which the Legislature declared to be wholly or partly "in a disturbed condition," the central administration was to intern hostages chosen from among the relatives of émigrés and rebels and the nobles excluded from civic rights; in the event of the murder of an active or retired government official, a soldier, or a purchaser of national property, the Directory would deport four hostages; what is more, all were collectively liable to a fine and responsible for paying indemnities to the victims' families as well as all other damages. An amnesty was offered to the rebels, with the exception of the leaders, on condition that they handed over their arms; if they failed to take advantage of this offer, they would be summoned before a military commission and executed upon identification.

Finally, that same 24 Messidor, Montpellier presented his report on the legal proceedings that the Councils, the Jacobin papers and the constant flow of addresses kept demanding against Reubell, La Revellière, Merlin, Treilhard, the ministers, and the commissioners to the armies; it concluded in favor of indicting the four Directors and Schérer. The Five Hundred accepted the report, but as the law laid down certain formalities which had to take thirty-three days before the matter was even referred to the Ancients, there was time for resistance to be organized.

At the end of Messidor, it was already strong, and on the twenty-sixth, the anniversary of the fourteenth of July, Sieyès issued an initial warning to the Jacobins. It was not that he, any more than the Directorials in the Councils, was opposed to measures of public safety, but they were all determined, whatever the cost, to keep the enforcement of such measures in their own hands; what frightened them was that the Jacobins declared that these measures would remain vain if the old revolutionary spirit was not awakened among the common people; this suggested that before long they would insist on associating the people with the government and that France would witness, at the very least, the return of the revolutionary Committees. As early as the evening of 30 Prairial, Boulay had rejected as "an atrocious slander" the suggestion that the adversaries of the defunct Directory wanted to restore the 1793 regime: "No, no, it will never rise again; there is not one of us who would not die fighting any factionists who tried to bring it back." A little earlier, a report already quoted, recommending the dispatch of agents into the provinces to infuse fresh energy into the administration—in other words a return to one of the expedients often used after the tenth of August—added: "These agents wish to be received only into the class of honest, well-to-do people . . . they must be the protectors of persons and property."

This expressive text was answered by another, by Lamarque, from the other side: "Some want the people to be used to repel the barbarians; others are afraid of using that omnipotent force, in other words they dread the mass of the Republicans more than the hordes from the north."

The *levée en masse* and requisitioning undoubtedly increased fear and irritation throughout the country, but they were liveliest in the ranks of the upper middle class, the only class affected by the compulsory loan. Moreover, the contractors had been specially singled out for attack in a resolution of 5 Messidor, admittedly rejected by the Ancients, which had forbidden anyone in official or government employment to have any connection with their contracts. However, Lindet had persuaded a certain number of contractors and bankers to accept a treasury arrangement which liquidated part of the expected yield from the loan. The former accepted assignment of the loan up to the sum of thirty million francs in exchange for the assignments on the public coffers that they possessed, which the bankers, grouped in "syndicates," accepted as security for bills subscribed by themselves in favor of the government, which had them discounted or used them in payment. Perregaux also set a good example by putting his own name down for a large contribution to the loan. But, generally speaking, recriminations and passive resistance foreshadowed failure, and little more than a third of the expected sum was collected. A considerable number of rich people left Paris after dismissing their staff; and, as an even more significant sign of the times, it was announced that some factories were going to close. There can be no doubt that a compulsory loan, especially in such circumstances, was bound to produce a reduction in business; in this panic, there was also an element of genuine fear, and it is consequently impossible to tell how far political calculation entered into it; but political calculation is always present.

The Directory and its supporters were chiefly concerned about the legal proceedings which threatened the victims of the thirtieth of Prairial, for if they were carried out, matters would not end there. Barras and above all Sieyès were already under attack. Of the latter, it was alleged in conversation and in print that he had signed an agreement in Berlin obtaining the mediation of Prussia, in return for the surrender of some or all the Republic's conquests and the restoration of the Monarchy in favor of the Duc d'Orléans or the Duke of Brunswick. It is not known whether there was any substance in these allegations; in any case they terrified Sieyès.

Most of the newspapers had immediately launched an attack on the Messidor laws, and pamphlets and lampoons joined in; the left-wing deputies and their friends did not always refrain from provocative demonstrations, such as Jourdan's toast on July 14 "to the resurrection of the pikes"; slander and abuse were used in reply. The clubs, and especially the Club du Manège, were denounced as dens of crime and conspiracy; the *jeunesse dorée* came and threatened the Manège, whose members retaliated; the two sides came to blows. In several towns, such as Rouen, Amiens, and Caen, similar disturbances occurred; at Bordeaux, blood was shed.

Although its adversaries evoked the memory of the thirty-first of May, the Left could not count on a mass movement; there was no longer any popular municipality in Paris, nor any Sections, nor any armed force other than the garrison, about 20,000 men who had been quartered in the capital since the eighteenth of Fructidor. It was insinuated that the Jacobins wanted to stir up the suburbs, but when, by some extraordinary chance, they happened to formulate a program—as did Bach, for example, on 30 Thermidor at the Club du Manège, or Jourdan, on 27 Fructidor at the tribune—none of the social elements of the policy of Year II figured in it, except for the opening of workshops for the unemployed, which was simply a measure of assistance. True, hostility to the rich was apparent in items such as the reduction of large stipends and a war tax to which they alone were liable—measures which the Legislature had in fact already adopted—but there was nothing in all this to incite the populace to take up arms, and indeed it did not budge. The only precaution that it was imperative for the government to take was to put the majority on guard against taking fresh exceptional measures and, by means of a determined attitude, to prevent it from disintegrating. This is what Sieyès set about doing right away.

On 8 Thermidor (July 26), Cornet, one of his confedererates, suddenly got the Ancients to decide that no political society should henceforth be allowed within the precincts of the Legislature, as a result of which the Club du Manège moved into the church in the rue du Bac. But, after Cornet, Danton's tiresome friend Courtois had vehemently denounced the terrorists and asserted that they were planning to assassinate the Directors and summon a Convention. A commission was set up to examine the evidence; on the thirteenth, Cornet, the *rapporteur*, found nothing to report save a couple of posters that were declared to be seditious; but nonetheless he called upon the Directory to "enforce the Constitution." Two days before, the Ministry of Police had been entrusted to Fouché, and on 24 Thermidor (August 11), Marbot, who had been dismissed, was replaced by

Lefebvre. That same day, the final debate on the indictments began in the Five Hundred: it was the moment for
action. On the twenty-sixth, Fouché closed the club; and
on 1 Fructidor (August 18), the proposed indictments were
rejected by 217 votes to 214, which suggests that they might
well have been approved if the waverers had not been
intimidated by the blow that Sieyès had just struck. The
peace had not been disturbed, and the violent recriminations of the Left had no effect. From then on, nothing more
was heard of the clubs. The break between Sieyès and the
Jacobins was now absolute, and Barras, now compromised
in their eyes, found himself isolated. The Left, incidentally,
did not regard the battle as completely lost, and on two
occasions the Royalists' rebellion and military setbacks provided it with opportunities to resume the attack.

The signal for an insurrection was given on 18 Thermidor (August 5), in the Haute-Garonne and the neighboring
cantons, by ex-General Rougé and the Comte de Paulo. It
was formidable, and Toulouse was cut off for a while, but
it remained an isolated phenomenon; in the west, Bourmont
did not appear until the end of August, and he fixed the
taking up of arms for mid-October. The rebels of the south-
west were gradually scattered; those who held out were
routed at Montréjeau on 1 Fructidor (August 18). In Paris,
feeling had run high. Destrem brought the news to the Five
Hundred on 26 Thermidor, just as the club was being
closed. Domiciliary visits were promptly authorized for a
period of one month; subsequently, a "disturbed state"
was declared in a good many cantons, though it does not
seem that the Law of Hostages was effectively enforced
in them. Sieyès for his part, on 16 Fructidor (September
2) obtained the deportation of the staff of thirty-four Roy-

alist papers still affected by the law of 19 Fructidor, Year
V; but he took the opportunity to hit out in both directions:
the next day, another decree was issued for the arrest for
conspiracy of the staff of sixteen other papers, and this time
the Jacobin organs figured on the list. The majority had
been so thoroughly incited against the Jacobins that it had
forgotten its grievances against the Directory as a result.
The Ancients accordingly rejected the resolutions of 9 Messidor which were directed against the Directory, and notably that which forbade it to keep troops inside the constitutional belt without a special law; Sieyès was able to
retain them in order to carry out the *coup d'état* of the
eighteenth of Brumaire.

Meanwhile, in Italy, Joubert had taken the offensive
against Suvoroff, to the north of Genoa, without waiting
for Championnet, who was coming down into Piedmont,
to join him. On 28 Thermidor (August 15), at Novi, he
was killed and his defeated army was withdrawn by Moreau. However, this fresh disaster made less of an impression than the landing by the English at The Helder on 10
Fructidor (August 27); the Batavian fleet surrendered without a fight, 25,000 Russians were landed, and the Duke of
York arrived to take command. Daëndels and Brune were
pushed back and thrown onto the defensive. In Paris, a
new invasion was seen to be possible if the enemy pushed
south fast, and there was considerable alarm. In the Five
Hundred, on the twenty-seventh (September 13), Jourdan
solemnly proposed that the country should be declared to
be in danger. Tumult broke out, and the public galleries
joined in the commotion: this was the last of those dramatic
sessions that had studded the history of the Revolution.
Lucien Bonaparte turned against the Jacobins, and Daunou

put the majority on its guard with great political acumen, pointing out that either the declaration was merely sheer rhetoric, or else it would be invoked later on to obtain measures which the history of the Legislative Assembly and the Convention had made all too familiar. Boulay finally obtained an adjournment, which made it easy to predict the result. Meanwhile the mob had gathered at the Tuileries and everyone was wondering what Bernadotte would do. The Jacobins had gone and offered him great "authority" if he intervened in their favor. Despite all his bragging, he was afraid of risks and had decided to wait and see. But Sieyès acted boldly and, in agreement with Barras and Roger-Ducos, sent word to him that the Directory accepted the resignation he had not offered. The fact remained that the Jacobins, instead of appealing to the people, had also turned to the generals; the drama was nearing its end. On 28 Fructidor, Jourdan's motion was rejected by 245 votes to 171. However, a few days later, Garrau succeeded in getting the death penalty prescribed for anyone who proposed, supported, or even accepted any offer involving the dismemberment of the territory or a change in constitution. This was the last success the Left won.

All of a sudden, in fact, some resounding victories were obtained which completely changed the situation. Thugut had not wanted the Anglo-Russian forces to occupy the Netherlands by themselves, and had ordered the Archduke Charles to go and join them, leaving Switzerland to Korsakoff who had just arrived there with 28,000 Russians. Suvoroff would go and join his compatriot, thus leaving the Austrians in sole control of Italy. Paul I, proud of his role as liberator of Switzerland, accepted this splendid plan. The Archduke sensed the dangers it involved and tried in vain, on August 17, to crush Masséna before setting off. After a French attack had likewise failed, on the thirtieth, he had to resign himself to obeying, but he left his second in command, Hotze, on the Linth, while Korsakoff guarded the Limmat. Meanwhile, however, Lecourbe had reconquered the Gotthard Pass and the valley of the Reuss, and Molitor had advanced as far as Glaris, a move which blocked Suvoroff's way. Thus temporarily covered in the rear, Masséna, immediately after the Archduke's departure, attacked Korsakoff; the latter, surrounded in Zürich, escaped with difficulty, while Soult routed the corps under Hotze, who was killed. The second Battle of Zürich had lasted three days, from 3 to 5 Vendémiaire, Year VIII (September 25-27, 1799). Meanwhile Suvoroff had pushed Lecourbe back step by step as far as Altdorf. There, for want of a route along the lake, he had to cut across the mountains, and came up against Mortier, whom Masséna came hurrying up to support. The Russians turned upon Molitor, who, pushed back against the Linth, repulsed every attack at Näfels. Learning at last of the disaster that had overtaken Hotze, Suvoroff escaped by way of the Col de Panix, across the Tödi, and reached the Rhine on October 7 at Ilanz, whence he moved on to the Vorarlberg. The whole of Switzerland found itself once more in the hands of the French.

In Holland, the Duke of York had vainly attacked Brune at Bergen and Castricum, on September 19 and October 6. Because his troops were decimated by epidemics, he signed an evacuation agreement at Alkmaar on the eighteenth.

These victories were crowned by a piece of news which

seemed positively miraculous: on 17 Vendémiaire (Octobe.
9), Bonaparte had landed at Fréjus and was traveling toward Paris, arousing enthusiasm all the way. The return of
the Invincible One completed the general conviction that
the Republic had been saved. Since the beginning of the
war, the sequence had always been the same: defeat called
forth extreme measures; victory made them useless; in the
period of peril, the Jacobins imposed themselves because
they were bold and ruthless; when the danger had passed,
the moderates triumphed at small cost to themselves. The
reaction accordingly began. The Five Hundred appointed
commissions to examine the changes to be made in the
Law of Hostages and the legislation on the émigrés. The
Ancients rejected the Garrau resolution. Even more significant was the report which Thibault read out on 9 Brumaire
(October 31) on the compulsory loan, which he proposed
abolishing by increasing direct taxation by half. The Assembly voted in favor of printing the report, and Lesage-
Senault exclaimed: "The counterrevolution has been carried
out." The debate continued on the sixteenth and seventeenth, and was adjourned to the eighteenth, which was the
day of the *coup d'état*.

The crisis of Year VII had clearly been surmounted.
The Directory was in full command of the situation; the
exceptional laws were going to be repealed or modified; the
rich felt reassured; the danger of invasion had passed. But
for how long? After such a sore trial, was the country going
to wait for the spring campaign and the elections of Year
VIII to provoke a fresh crisis?

CHAPTER FIFTEEN

The Eighteenth of Brumaire

The crisis had been surmounted, but, of the perils that had produced it, not a single one had disappeared. In the spring, the war would begin again with all its hazards. And now that the armies had been brought back to the frontiers, where would the money come from? The government officials and the rentiers were crying famine, and all the public services were in abeyance. At home, the civil war had begun again. On October 14, at a signal given by Bourmont, the Chouans had seized Le Mans; then it was the turn of Nantes and Saint-Brieuc. Their successes were ephemeral; in Vendée, Travot promptly put down the rebellion, and to the north of the Loire, Hédouville was soon able to negotiate a peace; but the fact remained that the counterrevolution was still a threat. Among the politicians, the elections of Year VIII were the chief preoccupation. The reaction could play the Royalists' game; all the same, immediately after the Messidor laws, the Jacobins remained the principal bogymen. In any case, the uncertainty was nerve-racking: people were appalled at the idea that everything would begin all over again the following year. Finally, what was to be done about Bonaparte? Arriving in Paris on October 14, he showed a thoroughly Republican tact and visited the Institut like an ordinary ideologue. However, all eyes were turned on him. Nobody thought of blaming him for the Egyptian adventure; exiled by the wicked Directors, he had foiled their plot by the prodigious feat of miraculously avoiding Nelson twice over. He clearly had a lucky star, and nobody cared very much what position he was given, provided he took action. After Campo-Formio, he had been the government's adviser; now he could be entrusted with the conduct of the war as supreme commander. Would he be content with so little? Legally, he was too young to be a Director or a minister.

The need to revise the Constitution therefore became more pressing every day. Since the eighteenth of Fructidor, the number of people advocating revision had grown steadily. The triumvirs, not daring to carry it out in France, had nonetheless revealed their opinion by drawing up for the sister republics constitutions that introduced the Constitution of Year III only in a profoundly modified form. In the Five Hundred, on 2 Pluviôse, Year VI (January 22, 1798), one deputy went so far as to declare that the Constitution contained "the seeds of death." Daunou, in approving the twenty-second of Floréal, urged La Revellière to make arrangements to obtain favorable election results "until such time as the change in the personnel of the Legislature can be made less frequent"; on 10 Brumaire, Year VIII (November 1, 1799), the *Décade* published an openly revisionist article which has been attributed to him, and it is probable that by this time he had stopped considering a constitutional procedure, since he was one of the leading Brumairians. Outside the Councils, Benjamin Constant had adopted the same attitude, immediately after the eighteenth of Fructidor, and Madame de Staël likewise, notably in the pages which have been published in our own time under the title of *Fragments politiques*. But the revisionist *par excellence* was Sieyès, seeing that in Year III he had set his own plan against the one which had been adopted. Since then, his ideas had developed, though admittedly we know them only from conversations held after the *coup d'état*, of which Boulay, Daunou, and Roederer have left summaries, which incidentally are partially contradictory.

Since an immediate revision of the Constitution was legally impossible, a *coup d'état* was necessary and Sieyès had been considering it ever since his election. Even if the majority in the Councils had thought it to be indispensable, it would never have agreed to take the initiative. The *coup d'état* would therefore have to be military and anti-parliamentarian, as on the eighteenth of Fructidor; but this time it was a much chancier affair. In Year V, the army had expelled the Royalists with a will, but now the circumstances were entirely different; true, it did not like the "lawyers," but even so, they were Republicans and even Jacobins. To obtain its support, a leader was needed who had not only a brilliant reputation but also an irreproachable revolutionary record. On both scores there was nobody superior to Bonaparte, and chance had brought him along at exactly the right moment. The Jacobins had welcomed him just as eagerly as the rest, and, it seems, were putting out feelers to him. They would not have given him a free hand any more than the Royalists, and he rejected their advances. For what he wanted to do, he had to have the economic and social power of the notables at his service, whereupon having joined forces with him, they would be his prisoners, out of fear of the counterrevolution and of democracy. Besides, it was impossible for him to hesitate: he was a mere general on half-pay—whose situation was indeed of dubious legality—and he could not take command in Paris unless he found accomplices in the Directory and the Councils. The trouble was that he could not stand Barras (there was Joséphine between them, if nothing else) and he loathed Sieyès; Talleyrand had to intervene to square matters between him and the latter. Cambacérès, the Minister of Justice, was apparently in on the secret; it seems that Fouché was not initiated, but, discovering what was going on, made himself an officious accomplice. In the Ancients, President Lemercier and the inspectors of the hall played a decisive role; the Five Hundred were a doubtful quantity, but they had been persuaded to choose Lucien Bonaparte as their President. Some of the generals, such as Jourdan and Augereau, held themselves aloof; they could not intervene if the government was opposed to the idea. Most of them, however, rallied joyfully to Bonaparte in order to gain control of the Republic; Moreau himself was so full of rancor that he was prepared to help the man who was to bring about his ruin. Collot, the contractor, advanced a little money, and he was probably not the only one; on 7 Brumaire (October 29), a law had suspended the assignments that had been made to them until their accounts were audited; in the evening of the nineteenth, they were handed over to them.

To justify the enterprise, a terrorist plot was alleged; and, since the fear which the terrorists inspired had gripped the bourgeoisie since the ninth of Thermidor, the eighteenth of Brumaire, in this respect, can already be seen as the culmination of the period. This accusation, made in bad faith, did not meet with much incredulity, for since Messidor most of the papers had been making it. Madame de Staël bears witness to the extent to which the possibility of a Jacobin victory terrified people:

> I was so convinced that, in that event, one could expect the cruelest persecution, that I gathered together all the money which I then had with my men of business in order to divide it between two of my closest friends and myself, so that we could immediately go abroad. Every quarter of an hour, I received news from Saint-Cloud, and, depending on the news I received, I hastened or postponed my departure.

However, some of the representatives could be expected to ask for proof of the existence of the alleged plots; they would also object that the Directory was sufficiently well protected, as had been shown since Year IV, and that in any case it was for the Directory to ask the Councils for exceptional measures, at the same time informing them of the facts. An extraordinary meeting of the Ancients was therefore called, and it was arranged that those likely to be troublesome should be informed too late. On 18 Brumaire (November 9), Cornet mounted the tribune, and, after hearing his account of the imminent peril, those present voted the agreed measures: the transfer of the Councils to Saint-Cloud (which was legal), and the appointment of Bonaparte as commander of the troops in Paris (which was not, for only the Directory had the right to make an appointment of this sort). From that moment, the battle had been won. Already, Bonaparte had brought the generals together at his house in the rue de la Victoire; the troops immediately set off. If there had been a majority in the Directory which had refused to recognize the Ancients' unconstitutional decision, it might have found a general to set against Bonaparte. Everything depended on Barras; he allowed himself to be persuaded to leave. Gohier and Moulin were powerless, and Moreau held them prisoners until they tendered their resignations.

At Saint-Cloud, the conspirators, it seems, were counting on the Councils to proclaim the overthrow of the Constitution of their own accord; but they had not prepared a scenario, or even a text which would provide the opportunity for debate. Consequently the plot very nearly came to grief. In the Ancients, those who had been absent the day before protested; the majority hesitated, all the more so since, from the legal point of view, the initiative lay with the Five Hundred where the Left was stubbornly holding out. Bonaparte decided to intervene. Addressing the Ancients, he once again denounced the plot without making any positive suggestions, and, in reply to voices invoking the Constitution, he retorted angrily: "The Constitution? You have violated it; it no longer exists." With the Five Hundred it was worse; at his entry, uproar broke out; by what right did he enter the Assembly without being summoned? The cry of "Outlaw him!" was heard. He turned pale and left the hall. A confused discussion followed. Lucien defended his brother and, rather than take a vote on the proposal to outlaw him, left the chair; some grenadiers burst into the hall and took him outside. The two Bonapartes, on horseback, went and harangued the troops, Lucien denouncing the factious deputies who had sold themselves to England, and who had dared to hurl themselves upon their general to stab him with their daggers. The Guard of the Legislature was itself finally won over, and, while the charge was being sounded, forced the Five Hundred, who were still deliberating, to evacuate the Orangerie.

That evening, a small number of deputies, who had been gathered together with considerable difficulty, organized the provisional Consulate. Contrary to expectations, there was some resistance: it was proposed that the meeting of the Councils be adjourned until 1 Nivôse, when they would elect a new Directory. But the Brumairians won the day easily. The Councils, some of whose members were in any case declared to have been expelled, were replaced by two commissions whose function was to pass the laws proposed by the Consuls and to prepare a new Constitution. The three Consuls were Bonaparte, Sieyès and Roger-Ducos: they were said to be equal, but there could be no doubt about the true state of affairs. It was not only a day of lies —the fiction of the daggers added to that of the plot—but also a day of dupes; since the civilians had not been sufficiently docile, the soldiers had had to be given free rein, and as a result Bonaparte had promptly and finally eclipsed Sieyès. The eighteenth of Brumaire is therefore usually represented as the occasion of Bonaparte's accession to power. Nonetheless, however dazzling his reign may have been, that *journée* had a wider historical significance.

By the Constitution of Year III, the Thermidorians had tried to re-establish, in a Republican form, the liberal representative regime which the bourgeoisie had attempted to inaugurate in 1789, and which is one of the characteristic features of its preponderance. The history of the Directory is that of the gradual failure of this attempt; in point of fact, the Republic had been reduced once more to a dictatorship. Putting an end to all ambiguity, the eighteenth of Brumaire made it possible to organize that dictatorship by the abolition of elections and the omnipotence of the Executive.

The events of the period make it abundantly clear why the annual recurrence of elections should have become intolerable to the Directorials. Moreover, they had no lack of objective motives, for, if frequent elections can be seen as an indispensable corrective for a purely representative system, since they alone enable the citizens to exercise their sovereignty, it is also true that they weary the citizens themselves and are prejudicial to the efficiency of both government and administration, making them unstable and monopolizing their attention. Annual elections, however, only aggravated the fundamental defect that the Montagnards had pointed out in the electoral system: the Revolution at war could not allow its enemies to turn freedom and elections against it, by promising peace and an end to the sacrifices which it had to impose for its own safety. That is why they had suspended the Constitution until the cessation of hostilities. Without ever admitting that the hated Jacobins were in the right, Thermidorians and Directorials had been obliged to make this admission implicitly with the decree of the two-thirds, and with the violation, on the eighteenth of Fructidor, of their own Constitution. To suspend it as in 1793 did not suit them, and would have left the future uncertain. The supporters of the divine right were still too powerful, inside and outside France, for them to think of repudiating the principle of the sovereignty of the people, in the name of which the bourgeoisie had seized power. As has often happened since, they had therefore looked for a device which would allow them to falsify the enforcement of that principle, and had tried it out on the twenty-second of Floréal; but, in Year VII, it had proved ineffective. That is why Sieyès, in the Constitution of Year VIII, decided to counterbalance election by means of co-optation. Already, the Constitution of Year III had resorted to this last method in order to complete the administrative bodies; everything considered, the decree of the two-thirds and the purge of the twenty-second of Floréal were substitutes for it; and Madame de Staël had advocated it for the recruitment of the Ancients. In Year VIII, the Brumairians installed themselves in the assemblies. In the future, the people would present them only with candidates; their dictatorship became permanent.

The Montagnards had not confined themselves to suspending elections; they had also concentrated and stabilized the Executive, stretching its powers to the limit. The Constitution of Year III had granted the Directory considerable authority; it had extended this on its own account, and the Councils themselves, carried away by circumstances, had conferred supplementary powers on it—powers which were on a temporary basis, but which were renewed so often that they had become practically normal as a result. From one end of the period to the other, the Executive, by its appointment of a considerable number of administrations and courts, by the extension of its statutory powers, by its police despotism and its contempt for the rights of the individual, had moved towards the Constitution of Year VIII.

However, the Convention had been jealous of its Committee of Public Safety and the Councils of the Directory. These executive organs were chosen by the Legislature; their collective character and the divisions which resulted from it had provoked or promoted their fall on the ninth of Thermidor and the thirteenth of Prairial. La Revellière deplored the fact that the Constitution of Year III had not granted the Directory the right of veto or, at the least, the power to initiate laws, the right of dissolution, and the control of the Treasury; his colleagues shared his opinion and had strengthened the Executive in Holland, Switzerland and Rome. The Brumairians, restricting the power to initiate laws to the Consuls alone, dividing the right of debate and vote among three assemblies, and instituting a constitutional check for the benefit of a conservative Senate, weakened the Legislature to such an extent that it was henceforth incapable of resistance; the subjection of which it had complained under the Directory was made absolute. The Consuls, appointed under the Constitution of Year VIII for ten years, and directly invested by a plebiscite, were on the contrary an independent power. What is more, unity was imposed upon the Executive, since the First Consul alone was entrusted with the power of decision. It was in this respect that the eighteenth of Brumaire was a day of dupes for Sieyès. Yet according to Fabre de l'Aude, he bitterly criticized the collective character of the Directory, as Carnot had done, maintaining that "a number of leaders lead nothing"; but he wanted "a dual mechanism" —"a head plus a sword to carry out what the head devises." His opinion did not prevail. Some Brumairians doubtless preferred to make sure of Bonaparte's favor, but men such as Cabanis and Daunou who never joined in the scramble for office, and who were sufficiently high-minded to consider nothing but the general good, must have felt that a single stable will was indispensable to the salvation of the Revolution, as Robespierre had believed. The evolution of the wartime Revolution toward a dictatorship thus reached its culminating point.

If the liberal experiment of the Constitution of Year III had turned out badly, the barrier it had set up against democracy had proved to be solid: power remained in the hands of the conservative bourgeoisie. However, the latter had considered itself in danger of Year VI and Year VII. Various remedies were envisaged, such as the raising of the franchise qualification, conditions of eligibility—above all the obligation for representatives to be landowners, as Boissy d'Anglas had suggested in Year III—and also graduality, which the Directory had introduced in Holland and Rome. But these restrictions, which would seem adequate in 1814, were not sufficient in Year VIII, because while they would bar the way to the Jacobins, the Royalists could not suffer from them. That is why co-optation was preferred. This solution bore the mark of its time: the monopoly of power was reserved exclusively for the notables, but they were at least notables. Since Year IV, a considerable volume of administrative work had been performed which, as we have seen, laid the foundations in many respects for that of the Consulate; thus it has rightly been said of the history of the Directory that, despite its detractors, it could take as its motto: *Sic vos, non vobis*. Under Bonaparte's eye, the bourgeoisie continued its work: it was the bourgeoisie that established the institutions of the Consulate and the Empire, and drew up the laws, thus fixing the limits of the society it dominated. The eighteenth of Brumaire consecrated the Revolution in the form in which the bourgeoisie had conceived it in 1789.

Yet the fact remains that it held terrible disappointments in store for that class. One was easy to foresee. In setting up a dictatorship aimed against its enemies, the bourgeoisie had not intended to abandon freedom for itself or to subject itself to despotic control; but, since the *coup d'état* had been carried out by the army, who could prevent its leader from perpetrating more? The Brumairians imagined that the conservative Senate would suffice to thwart him; on the contrary, it was the chief instrument of usurpation. But the people who were most disappointed were those who expected the eighteenth of Brumaire to lead to the abandonment of propaganda and even of that interpretation of the Constitution which, forbidding any cession of national territory, made a compromise peace impossible. In opposing the Garrau resolution, Porcher, in a little-known speech, had bluntly shown that he regarded as insane those who would not abandon some of their compatriots to the foreign yoke, in order to obtain peace; and the aforementioned article in the *Décade* blamed the Constitution for having, by declaring the frontiers sacrosanct, decreed perpetual war and "the annihilation of all the French people." These revisionists had no inkling of the invincible romanticism of the Napoleonic imagination!

But of all that that imagination dreamed or produced— a new dynasty, the partial restoration of the *ancien régime*, the European Empire—nothing has remained. What has endured is the predominance of the notables, the work they completed under his guidance, the final consolidation of the Revolution which, by making a dictatorship useless in the future, made it possible to begin the liberal experiment again in 1814. This is the real significance of the eighteenth of Brumaire: initiated by a few bold bourgeois, it finally established the power of the bourgeoisie.

BIBLIOGRAPHICAL SUGGESTIONS

No comprehensive study of the Directorial period has been written since the appearance, between 1895 and 1897, of *Le Directoire*, by L. SCIOUT, 4 vols. in-8°, which represented an advance in documentation, but which had been conceived as an indictment. A. AULARD, *Histoire politique de la Révolution* (1901; 5th ed., 1921), deals only with internal political history; the same is true of A. MEYNIER, *Les coups d'état du Directoire; Le 18 fructidor an V* (1927); *Le 22 floréal an VI* (1928); *Le 18 brumaire et la fin de la République* (1929). A. MATHIEZ, *Le Directoire*, posthumously published by J. GODECHOT (1933), does not go beyond the eighteenth of Fructidor. L. MADELIN deals with the history of the Directory only insofar as it concerns Bonaparte: *La jeunesse de Bonaparte* (1937); *L'ascension de Bonaparte* (1937). *Le Directoire et la paix de l'Europe* (1911) by R. GUYOT is a classic work, but deals only with foreign policy.

As a basis for study, see the chapters devoted to the Directory by G. PARISET in Vol. II of *L'Histoire de France contemporaine*, published under the direction of E. LAVISSE (1920); and by R. GUYOT in Vol. XIII of *Peuples et civilisations*, the collection published under the direction of L. HALPHEN & PHILIPPE SAGNAC (1930; 2nd ed., 1938); the new version of this last volume by G. LEFEBVRE (1951; 2nd ed., enlarged, 1956); G. GODE-CHOT, *La Grande Nation*, 2 vols. in-8° (1956); M. REINHARD, *Le Grand Carnot*, 2 vols. in-8° (1950, 1952).

For internal history, see: J. GODECHOT, *Les institutions de la France sous la Révolution et l'Empire* (1951); important articles by J. SURATTEAU in the *Annales historiques de la Révolution française; Les élections de l'an IV* (1951, 1952, 1955) and *Les élections de l'an V* (1957); M. REINHARD, *Le département de la Sarthe sous le régime directorial* (1935); R. SCHNERB, *Les contributions directes à l'époque de la Révolution dans le département du Puy-de-Dôme* (1933); *La dépression économique sous le Directoire* (*Annales historiques de la Révolution*, 1934); THÉRÈSE AUBIN, *Le rôle politique de Carnot depuis les élections de germinal an V jusqu'au coup d'état du 18 fructidor* (*Annales historiques de la Révolution française*, 1932); G. CAUDRILLIER, *L'association royaliste de l'institut philanthropique à Bordeaux et la conspiration anglaise en France pendant la seconde coalition* (1908); J. STERN, *Le mari de Mlle Lange: Michel-Jean Simons* (1933); E. DELCAMBRE, *La période du Directoire dans la Haute-Loire* (1940); *Le coup d'état jacobin du 18 fructidor et ses répercussions dans la Haute-Loire* (1942); *La vie dans la Haute-Loire sous le Directoire* (1943); G. COIRAULT, *Les écoles centrales dans le Centre-Ouest* (1940); CHARLES H. VAN DUZER, *The Contribution of the Ideologues to French Revolutionary Thought* (Baltimore, 1935); GEORGIA ROBISON, *Revellière-Lepeaux, Citizen Director* (New York, 1938); J. BOURDON, *Le mécontentement public et les craintes des dirigeants sous le Directoire* (*Annales historiques de la Révolution française*, 1946); J. GODECHOT, *Le Directoire vu de Londres* (*ibid.*, 1949-50).

For military history and foreign policy, see: H. BOURDEAU, *Les armées du Rhin au début du Directoire* (1909); G. VALLÉE, *La conscription dans le département de la Charente* (1937); J. GODE-CHOT, *Les commissaires aux armées sous le Directoire* (1937); *Les insurrections militaires sous le Directoire* (*Annales historiques de la Révolution française*, 1933); J. DROZ, *La pensée politique et morale des Cisrhénans* (1940). For Bonaparte's early career, as well as the aforementioned works by L. MADELIN, see:

J. Colin, *L'éducation militaire de Napoléon* (1900); Spenser Wilkinson, *The Rise of General Bonaparte* (Oxford, 1930); G. MacClellan, *Venice and Bonaparte* (Princeton, 1931); G. Ferrero, *Aventure: Bonaparte en Italie* (1936); see also the articles in the review *La Révolution française*: P. Muret, G. Ferrero, *historien de Bonaparte* (1937); G. Ferrero, *Bonaparte et l'Italie*, and P. Muret, *Encore quelques remarques sur l'Aventure de Mr G. Ferrero* (1938); D. Bernard, *Documents et notes sur l'histoire religieuse du Finistère sous le Directoire.*

See also: G. Lefebvre, *Napoléon* (Vol. XIV of the collection *Peuples et civilisations*, 1935; 2nd ed., 1941). The present work is a condensation of a course of lectures given at the Sorbonne.

GEORGES LEFEBVRE was born in France in 1874. At the age of fifty, he began his extensive publication on the French Revolution with a dissertation submitted for the degree of *Docteur ès lettres*. It consisted of four volumes on the rural sociology of the Department du Nord before and during the Revolution and was perhaps the longest doctoral dissertation ever written. Until his death in 1959, M. Lefebvre was Professor Emeritus of the History of the French Revolution at the University of Paris. His *Coming of the French Revolution*, first published in English in 1947 and now available in the Vintage paperback series, has become one of the most distinguished contributions to history written in the twentieth century. He is also the author of the definitive study, *The Thermidorians* (available in Vintage Books),which is a companion volume to *The Directory*.

VINTAGE HISTORY EUROPEAN

VINTAGE HISTORY—AMERICAN

A free catalogue of VINTAGE BOOKS *will be sent at your request. Write to* Vintage Books, 457 Madison Avenue, New York, New York 10022.

VINTAGE RUSSIAN LIBRARY

DUE

A free catalogue of _____ your request. Write
to Vintage Books, 4 _____ New York 10022.

PRINTED IN U.S.A.